Three Essays on Style

Erwin Panofsky

Three Essays on Style

Edited by
Irving Lavin

With a Memoir by
William S. Heckscher

The MIT Press
Cambridge, Massachusetts
London, England

Library of Congress Cataloging-in-Publication Data

Panofsky, Erwin, 1892–1968.
Three essays on style / Erwin Panofsky ; edited by Irving Lavin ; with a memoir by William S. Heckscher.
p. cm.
Includes two essays originally written in English and first published in German : Die ideologischen Vorläufer des Rolls-Royce-Kühlers & Stil und Medium im Film. Frankfurt, New York : Campus Verlag, 1993.
Includes bibliographical references and index.
Partial Contents: What is Baroque?—Style and medium in the motion pictures—The ideological antecedents of the Rolls-Royce radiator.
ISBN 0-262-16151-6
1. Art. I. Lavin, Irving, 1927– . II. Heckscher, William S. III. Title.
N7445.2.P36 1995
700—dc20
                                                          95-929
                                                          CIP

Contents

Preface

This book had its origin in the publication of German translations of two of the essays presented here, along with an introduction by myself (entitled "Panofskys Humor") and William Heckscher's memorial of Panofsky: Erwin Panofsky, *Die ideologischen Vorläufer des Rolls-Royce-Kühlers & Stil und Medium im Film. Mit Beiträgen von Irving Lavin und William S. Heckscher,* Frankfurt/New York: Campus Verlag, 1993. I am grateful to Campus Verlag for their cooperation. I have included here the previously unpublished lecture "What Is Baroque?" and an enlarged version of the introduction, which has benefitted from the thoughtful comments and criticisms of Ernst Kitzinger, Carl Schorske, Craig Smyth, and an anonymous reader. I am indebted to Gerda Panofsky for her kindness throughout the realization of this project; in particular, for granting permission to publish the lecture on Baroque art, and providing the successive manuscript versions of that work from her personal archive.

I. L.
Princeton
May 1994

Introduction

Irving Lavin

This volume brings together all but one of the papers devoted to the subject of style written by Erwin Panofsky in English after he moved to America, having been dismissed as a Jew from his professorship at the University of Hamburg. The first essay dates from 1934, the year of his immigration; the second was written in 1936, the third in 1962.[1] Despite their chronological spread, and apart from their relative unfamiliarity even to art historians, the three contributions have in common several distinguishing features within Panofsky's vast scholarly legacy. The qualities they share reveal essential, if unexpected, aspects of Panofsky's sensibility, both intellectual and personal. To begin with, the subjects differ radically from the methodological formula commonly associated with Panofsky in his later years, that is, iconology, narrowly defined as the analysis of subject matter in art. These essays are all about style, its character, its geography, and its history. Panofsky seeks to describe the visual symptoms endemic, as it were, to works of a certain period (Baroque), medium (film), or national entity (England), and to assess the significance of those symptoms in a larger, conceptual frame of reference. Style—the "visualness" of the visual arts—is, after all, the key issue in the legitimization of art history as an autonomous field of inquiry.[2] In this enterprise he was following in the footsteps of the preceding generation, which had laid the foundations of the modern discipline devoted to the nature, significance, and history of visual expression, and employing distinctive tools of analysis. Conspicuous among these pioneers were Alois Riegl and Heinrich Wölfflin, and Panofsky's way of thinking about the problem and many of his observations depend on their insights.[3] Questions of style in art history were still very much in vogue in the 1930s, when the first two essays were written, and remained so for the next twenty years or more. Thereafter, however, style went out of style. Indeed, style became rather a bad word after it was supplanted in the 1950s by the seemingly more concrete and intellectual rewards offered by Panofsky's own methodological trademark, iconology; the socially relevant art history of the 1970s and 1980s followed, to be continued in the multiculturalism of recent years. Only lately have there been signs of a revival of interest in style, and in this sense the essays may be said to possess once again a certain timeliness.[4]

A second common denominator is that all three essays are about matters of principle. Their very titles betray a bold, not to say brash, willingness to grapple with the most fundamental tasks that confront the historian:

in particular, how to make sense out of history by giving it structure and meaning. They deal with essential aesthetic dispositions—the "Baroque" nature of seventeenth-century art, the "filmic" nature of the art of the motion picture, the "English" nature of the art of the British Isles—that manifest the significance of style in different aspects: chronological, technical, ethnic. Panofsky believed that certain formal modes are "proper" to a given medium, that in a given time and place all works of art have certain features in common, despite individual and local variations, and that shifts from one such commonality to another—periodization, in other words—constitute the historical process. In our age of complexity and deconstruction, such an attitude may seem naive, or arrogant, or both. Yet, with training and experience (and a lot of mistakes, to be sure) art historians tend to be able to appreciate, date, and localize works of art just by looking at them. If we want to know why, we have to turn to the Wölfflins and Panofskys of the discipline for help.

A further point, of special significance with respect to Panofsky's own development, arises partly from the circumstance that the essays were not intended to be professional academic tracts but were conceived originally as public lectures for nonspecialist audiences, a fact that certainly conditioned both their content (broad topics of general interest) and their form (relatively brief and informal in tone).[5] However, it is also apparent that the choice of subjects and manner of treating them were affected by a particular turn of mind. The problems of style preoccupied Panofsky throughout his life; his first publication after his dissertation was a critique of Wölfflin titled "Das Problem des Stils in der bildenden Kunst."[6] Reflecting his debt to the preceding generation, his earlier works on the topic are more abstract and theoretical than these very concrete, historical demonstrations, which reflect the mental shift Panofsky experienced after coming to America. The same may be said of his one other post-immigration paper devoted specifically to style, the better-known *Gothic Architecture and Scholasticism*, a lecture published as a separate volume and still in print,[7] in which Panofsky correlates form and structure to a particular mode of reasoning and intellectual discourse. A change is also evident in Panofsky's approach to his subjects. In the first paper, he identifies and embraces as virtues certain egregious features of a great period style—sentimentality, frivolity, and even humor—that flouted the classical aesthetic canon and offended "serious" critics. In the second, he takes seriously a "frivolous" theme: the artistic development of a new, unabashedly popular, and commercial technique. In the third, he gives a frivolous spin to an idea that Panofsky had seen become, especially in his native country, deadly serious: the definition of the inherent character of a millennial national culture, the "genius" of a people. All these passionately felt and enchantingly devised arguments entail ironic inversions of conventional attitudes that might be expected from a traditional German historian of medieval and Renaissance art.

It is important to bear in mind in reading these essays that matters of style are central to many of Panofsky's other interests, such as proportion theory, perspective, even Galileo and the "design" of the planetary orbits.[8] Moreover, the subjects dealt with here also come up in other contexts: Dürer and the technique of engraving, national and period styles in German Romanesque sculpture, and early Netherlandish painting.[9] The role of style in Panofsky's thought is by no means encompassed by the writings devoted expressly to the subject.

Finally, before considering the essays individually, we may take note that two of them are the only occasions where Panofsky ventured into the domain of modern art: film and commercial design, the former in extenso, the latter en passant.[10]

Periodization is the underlying theme of the first work, whose significance may be gauged by the remarkable fact that the standard history of seventeenth- and early-eighteenth-century Italian art, Rudolf Wittkower's *Art and Architecture in Italy 1600–1750,* first published in 1958, constantly refers to the Baroque but never seeks to define the term or describe the general characteristics of the period that justify its use. The book is a magnum opus of erudition and art-historical perspicuity, and this conceptual silence bespeaks a certain shyness in the field as a whole with regard to what might be called high synthesis. The truth, I fear, is that while our knowledge of the Baroque has increased exponentially in the last half century, our understanding has not kept pace. What is Baroque, anyway? Many of us—and especially the specialists among us—if pressed to respond to that challenging question, would probably sputter, gasp, and take refuge in the formulations provided by our heroic pioneer, Heinrich Wölfflin, in his *Principles of Art History* (1915). But Wölfflin was defining the first principles of a new discipline, whereas we are professional practitioners, too sophisticated, perhaps, to discuss first principles. Whatever the reason, I believe that one of the most important, and fundamentally new, contributions to the topic since Wölfflin is contained in the lecture by Panofsky entitled "What Is Baroque?," which was written in 1934 and presented often for many years thereafter.[11] Panofsky never published the piece and ultimately came to regard it as obsolete.[12] I sometimes wonder, in fact, whether "What Is Baroque?" was one of those papers that, as I have heard, Panofsky deliberately withheld from publication in order to have something available for the flood of guest lecture invitations he received. A mimeographed text, evidently transcribed from Panofsky's typescript by a student at Vassar, where he gave the lecture at the conference in 1935, has always been available in various libraries, which is how I first encountered it when I was a graduate student at New York University's Institute of Fine Arts in the early 1950s.[13]

I have long thought that the text should be published, despite its shortcomings, and the author's misgivings, partly because it documents a distinctly "transitional" phase in Panofsky's own development—elegant English even at that early date in the American half of his life, yet with traces of the long, complicated Germanic periods that, as he later astutely observed, the need to adapt to Anglo-Saxon usage expunged from his prose style. More important, however, Panofsky's way of considering a perennial and quintessentially art-historical problem from a broad, interdisciplinary point of view makes the essay particularly consonant with current attitudes in the discipline. Indeed, because of this method, the implications of Panofsky's response look well beyond the narrow purview of his question.

To comprehend the significance of the substance of Panofsky's argument, it should be recalled that Wölfflin's analysis is based on a fundamental dichotomy between two opposing formal systems, classic and Baroque. The essence of his concept lies not only in the five antinomic components of the contrasting systems, but also in the notion that they are not temporally fixed; they represent immanent, immutable poles of perception, between which all artistic vision inevitably oscillates—not for nothing did he call his book *Principles of Art History*.[14] Panofsky also conceives of style and its development in dialectical terms, starting from an underlying dichotomy, an interior discrepancy he found embedded in the art of the early Renaissance. There was on the one hand a renewed interest in antiquity, and on the other hand a quite nonclassical interest in naturalism—epitomized by the importation to Florence and influence of Hugo van der Goes's Portinari altarpiece; there was on the one hand mathematical perspective, and on the other hand a persistent

Gothicism evident in the tendency of forms to cling to the picture plane. The great masters of the High Renaissance managed briefly to reconcile this dichotomy into a harmonious balance, which then disintegrated in the battlefield of contradictory forces, the everlasting tension, that pervaded mannerist culture. The burning of Giordano Bruno, Panofsky said, was an emphatically mannerist occurrence. In the Baroque, there was again a reconciliation. The conflicts and contrasts between plastic and spatial tendencies, ideal beauty and reality, neopagan humanism and Christian spiritualism, while still subsisting, began to merge. The merger was now in a new sphere, however, not in the harmonious balance and classical unity of the High Renaissance, but in highly subjective feelings, a picturesque play of light and shadow, deep, irrational space, and melting expressions. Panofsky described the Baroque as the paradise of the High Renaissance regained, but haunted and enlivened by the intense consciousness of an underlying dualism. The essence and novelty of the Baroque lies precisely in this twofold reconciliation of forces—an overwhelming feeling of subjective excitement, and an awareness of that feeling. While the hearts of seventeenth-century people quiver with emotion, he says, their consciousness stands part and "knows." The experience of many conflicts led to a kind of awakening. The Baroque, therefore, is not the decline of the Renaissance—at the time he wrote the paper, Panofsky later recalled, "the word 'Baroque' was still employed as a term of opprobrium in the Anglo-Saxon countries"[15]—but its climax: culture's inherent conflicts were overcome, and not by smoothing them away but by realizing them consciously and transforming them into productive energy. (This definition of cultural progress in terms of psychological conflict recognition and resolution sounds remarkably like an art-historical transfiguration of Freud. I am aware of no evidence connecting Panofsky to Freud or psychoanalysis, however.)

On the phenomenological level, Panofsky had little that was new to say about the manifestations of the historical evolution. His readings of the ingredients of Renaissance art—classical revival, new naturalism, lingering medievalism, the anxiety of early mannerism, the formulaic quality of later mannerism (now called the Maniera), the return around 1600 to naturalism, classicism, and the High Renaissance—were "in the air" by 1934:[16] indeed, I suspect that this element of "cooptation" may have been one of the reasons he never developed the talk for publication.[17] Two such borrowings interest me particularly as a student of Bernini: Panofsky's thoughts on the frontality of Baroque sculpture and the modernity of caricature reflect recent, pioneering studies by the then bright new star on the art-historical horizon, Rudolf Wittkower.[18]

Panofsky's contribution was to bring together these myriad, more or less isolated observations, reformulate them in his own image, and integrate them, via the process of contrast and reconciliation, into a coherent argument. The result was a comprehensive view that encompassed and gave focus to the entire development of European art from the Renaissance to the mid-nineteenth century (the death of Goethe, as he put it). Panofsky's view of the Baroque as part of one continuous arc of Western development that ended only with the Industrial Revolution and the rise of mass culture, anticipated much recent historical thought. Contemporary thinkers also share this reference to economic and social forces as effecting historical change. But it is striking and symptomatic of the particular way in which he perceived the contemporary relevance of his own work that he ends his talk with an ironically brooding observation: that the unknown God or Devil who brought an end to the humanistic tradition of the Renaissance threatens the very existence of humankind in our own time.[19]

On the level of principle, it is clear that Panofsky's process of thesis versus antithesis followed by synthesis was a Hegelian transfiguration of the bipolar principles of Riegl and Wölfflin. But there are three essential differences. First, Panofsky's principles were not purely formal modes, like Riegl's tactile and optic values, or Wölfflin's closed and open form; and they were certainly not aesthetic categories related to quality judgments or taste. Concepts like classical antiquity, Gothic and mannerism, balance and harmony versus tension and conflict, while they evoke or correspond to distinctive formal traits, are deeply embedded in the fabric of human society: war, religion, science, psychology, even—in the case of the Baroque—that special form of wit to which Panofsky here accords the name "humor." And unlike interpreters who sought to instrumentalize the Baroque in terms of such notions as theatricality, or the Jesuit Counter Reformation, Panofsky's categories are ultimately inseparable from the entire gamut of apparently coincidental cultural values and social responses that used to be called the spirit of an age, the zeitgeist.[20] Second, Panofsky's polarities are not independent categories of perception and thought—timeless, built-in structures of the mind. Instead, they are specifically timebound, historical conditions whose manifestations are determined by, or are at least consonant with, other domains of contemporary meaning and experience. And third, whereas Wölfflin had focused on the polar extremes between which our modes of perception inevitably ebbed and flowed, Panofsky was concerned with an evolutionary process embodied in the interaction between antipodes to create a sequence of more or less complete syntheses that differed profoundly from one to the next.

However insightful and stimulating many of his individual observations about works of art may be, and however grand and compelling his reconstruction of the developmental and cultural forces at work during the period, the essential originality of the essay lies in what is, in the end, its main theme, the *psychological* interpretation of Baroque style.[21] In Panofsky's view, the Baroque left many valuable and lasting effects on Western civilization, but with this basic yet subtle thought he gave a positive cast even to the very "defects" of the style, such as sentimentality and frivolity. His definition was a penetrating extension into personal, even depth psychology of his notion of the Renaissance as the achievement of individual autonomy and historical distance. In this sense, the Baroque signaled the birth of modern European consciousness. In an unprecedented way, Baroque people were aware of their own feelings, including their own shortcomings, and were prepared to undertake uncompromising examinations of the self, whether through the critical philosophy of Descartes or a satirical portrait sketch by Bernini. Combining in one historical equation the concept of the Baroque with such disparate factors as the analysis of mind, swooning saints, frivolous angels, light and shade, deep space, frontally placed sculptures, and the invention of caricature drawing—all this becomes much more than a scintillating display of associations and ideas: the underlying theme of this "lordly racket," as Panofsky called it, portends nothing less than a new phase in human history. To define an epoch of history in terms of its psychological state, to define the nature of that state as one of *emotional* self-awareness, and to define that emotional self-awareness as peculiarly modern—all this seems to me an unparalleled act of historical imagination and insight.

In the film essay, the interrelation between style and material or technique is at issue. The article was published in three versions: initially in 1936 with the title "On Movies"; again the following year, slightly enlarged and with a new title, "Style and Medium in the Moving Pictures"; and a decade later in the definitive version, extensively revised and expanded and with the word "Moving" in the title changed to "Motion," when it was described as "one of the most significant introductions to the aesthetics of the motion picture yet to be written."[22] Already reprinted at least twenty-two times, it is by far Panofsky's most popular work, perhaps the most popular essay in modern art history. This unexampled success is the more astonishing given the author's traditional training and otherwise almost exclusive preoccupation with traditional "high" art. In fact, the essay offers a rare, if not unique, instance in which a sensitive and informed "eye- (and later 'ear-') witness" comments extensively on the evolution of a revolutionary new technical invention into a high art. Panofsky himself cites as a comparable innovation in the history of human communication the development of printmaking in the fifteenth century, but we have no comparable analysis of its nature and significance by a contemporary observer.[23]

Panofsky displays an amazing fund of knowledge—of plots, actors, directors, producers, filmic devices—which he obviously accumulated from an early age. He remembered the only *Kino* ("obscure and faintly disreputable") in all Berlin in 1905, when he was thirteen, and he watched the medium develop from its earliest infancy as a technical curiosity to a major international industry of great technical and artistic virtuosity. In this essay, therefore, the private-life experience of an avid moviegoer becomes part of the intellectual armament of a supremely articulate historian and theoretician of art. The circumstances of its origin are of great importance: it was not a formal presentation to a scholarly audience, but a casual talk delivered in 1934 to a group of Princeton amateurs intent on founding a film archive (ultimately one of the greatest in the world) at the Museum of Modern Art in New York.[24] Panofsky elsewhere describes himself as having been then a lecturer at New York and Princeton Universities; he had just settled permanently in Princeton, and the following year he was appointed to the nascent Institute for Advanced Study.[25] The occasion marked the rapport Panofsky had established with the liberal-minded, public-spirited, and WASPish social and cultural ambient then in the process of creating the portentous amalgam of European sophistication and American enthusiasm that would establish New York as a new world cultural center of modernism.[26]

The genial, peculiarly American context from which the essay arose is reflected in its original title, "On Movies." This distinctly colloquial American term, which has no real counterpart in other languages,[27] expressed the two essential points of Panofsky's conception of the medium and its development, one social, the other aesthetic. Panofsky lays great stress at the outset on the fact that film was first and foremost a medium of popular entertainment, devoid of aesthetic pretension, which reestablished the "dynamic contact between art production and art consumption" that is "sorely attenuated, if not entirely interrupted, in many other fields of artistic endeavor." The "movies" were a genuine "folk art," and if they rose to the level of high art they did so largely by never losing their common touch. This unpretentious social aspect of Panofsky's definition of the film is the substantive counterpart of his choice of the colloquial name for the medium.

The second principle on which Panofsky's analysis is based corresponds to the aesthetic aspect of his title, movement. The essence of the medium lies in its having given movement to a record of the real world, an observation that, as he admits, seems banal until he states and proceeds to develop his binary definition of the motion picture as the "dynamization of space" and the "spatialization of time." Although he does not say so explicitly, it is evident that this formulation suggesting an endemic interdependence of space and time, a sort of space-time continuum, owed much to the theory of relativity. An important corollary, however, is the integration of sound into this matrix, the spoken word being fatefully wedded to movement through the device of the close-up. Panofsky defines this sound-movement dimension of the space-time continuum as the "principle of coexpressibility." Much of the remainder of the essay is devoted to exploring the implications of these principles, including the dangers inherent in disregarding them, much like those attendant upon neglecting the roots of the medium in popular culture.

In the third, final version of the paper two complementary changes were introduced. The trace of colloquialism that remained in the "Moving" of the second title was replaced by the purely formal "Style and Medium in the *Motion* Pictures," which focuses entirely on the relationship between the technical properties of film and its expressive qualities. In the text, the social characterization retains its place, with some changes in wording at the beginning, but it becomes a kind of prelude to the now greatly expanded section dealing with the nature of the medium itself. The personal chat on a modern form of entertainment was thus transformed into a proper theoretical essay on a form of modern art. Balance is restored, however, in the last paragraphs, which deal with two points that lie at the crux of the matter: film's relation to society based on its commercial nature, and its relation to physical reality based on its technical nature. The requirement of communicability imposed by the first relationship and the requirement of realism imposed by the second are the preconditions for style in this uniquely modern medium.

To call the film essay "proper" is rather misleading, however. The title and the content are more ambitious than in the original version, but perhaps the most important quality of the text remained undiminished: the whole argument, full of erudite references to old and new films as well as to works of traditional art, is presented with an impish grace and wit wholly in keeping with the popular nature of the theme as Panofsky conceived it. Panofsky moves between Betty Boop and Buster Keaton with the same breathtaking ease born of intimate knowledge as he does between Albrecht Dürer and the Gothic cathedral. The prose combines the urbanity and entertainment value of the *New Yorker* magazine with the philosophical depth and methodological rigor of a German university treatise. Even in its ultimate form, then, the essay hovers in a sort of genre limbo somewhere between personal reminiscence, high journalism, formal art criticism, and professional art history. From any of these points of view it is a rogue, and it marks the birth of a new literary star—in English, no less!

The Rolls-Royce radiator raised for Panofsky the question of the ethnic component of style. While both the title and the content of the paper are remarkable, still more remarkable is the relationship between the two. Nowadays, the title would suggest something in the nature of a sociological disquisition on the taste and luxury of the English upper class, but one would be disappointed on two counts. The structure of English society is mentioned only incidentally, and the Rolls-Royce is mentioned only in the last, very brief paragraph. The body of the work is an audacious attempt to define the basic principle that inhabits English art, as well as other aspects of English culture, from the early Middle Ages through the nineteenth century. Panofsky again finds an "antinomy of opposite principles," comprising here "a highly subjective emotionalism" that may even be termed "romantic," and "a severely formal rationalism." He relates this bipolarity—as an incidental analogy, not as a causative "explanation"—to the peculiar "fact that social and institutional life in England is more strictly controlled by tradition and convention, yet gives more scope to individual 'eccentricity' than anywhere else."

The fact that Panofsky engaged in this enterprise at all is profoundly rooted in his heritage of continental, especially German art history. Two major books, both by German scholars, had been devoted to the Englishness of

English art, though curiously enough Panofsky does not refer to either of them: Dagobert Frey's *Englisches Wesen in der bildenden Kunst* (Stuttgart and Berlin, 1942, 496 pages) and Nikolaus Pevsner's *The Englishness of English Art* (New York, 1956, 208 pages). These works reflect, as does Panofsky's, a long tradition of characterological study, both individual and national, traceable to the eighteenth century and beyond. The pursuit of such ethnic and geographical taxonomies of style in art was a special preoccupation of German scholars of that generation.[28] England evidently presented a particular temptation for them, partly for substantive reasons—its insularity and the pronounced individuality of its artistic traditions—and partly no doubt also for its Anglo-Saxon "snob appeal." Despite wide differences in their approaches, moreover, all three studies have certain elements in common, methodologically and conceptually. All three perceive and define the essential character of English culture in terms of opposing, though occasionally amalgamated, forces of subjectivity and objectivity, intuition and rationality, romanticism and classicism, naturalness and order, and so forth. All three relate this dichotomy to extra-artistic factors such as the character of Britain's society, geography, and racial mix.[29]

Panofsky's essay differs from its precedessors in many ways, not least being its brevity. To be sure, it was presented in the form of a lecture at the American Philosophical Society, America's oldest and most sedate scientific society.[30] But the vast cultural panorama Panofsky evokes in a series of miraculously encapsulated surveys of English eighteenth-century gardens and architecture, medieval miniature painting, architecture, and literary sources— in that order—is an essential factor in the persuasiveness of his argument. The brilliant concatenation of ideas, illustrations, and texts presented in epigrammatic formulations carries the bedazzled reader with dizzying speed to an abrupt halt before the concluding paragraph. At this point the Rolls-Royce radiator appears, with its severely classical Greek temple-front grille improbably surmounted by the curvaceous romantic windblown Victory of Samothrace, alias the "Silver Lady." The very incongruity of this design becomes the inevitable epitome, the trademark par excellence, of everything it means to be English. Perhaps the most beguiling aspect of the essay, in fact, is precisely that the climax of an utterly serious and penetrating analysis of a major European culture is, to use Panofsky's favorite word for things ironic but profound, "amusing."

I hope that two salient characteristics of Panofsky's style, intellectual and literary, will have emerged from this brief consideration of his own discussions of style. The first is that whether the subject is periodization, technique, or geo-ethnicity, Panofsky, unlike his predecessors, is never a pure formalist. Style for him inevitably has an expressive role, and he constantly invokes the subject matter of works of art, their "iconography"—be it the new conception of martyrdom scenes in the Baroque, the narrative possibilities of the animated cartoon, or the "angelic" intricacies of the evangelist portraits in an Irish illuminated book. Indeed, it might be said that Panofsky's primary concern—his ultimate heuristic principle of interpretation—was to illustrate how style or expressive form lends meaning to subject matter, and thus relates the work of art to the full range of extrastylistic factors that condition its creation.[31] After all, this interrelationship between style and meaning lies at the heart of perhaps his most familiar, and still indispensable, historical formulation: that of the Renaissance as having achieved, after the destruction of Greco-Roman civilization, the reintegration of classical form with classical content.[32]

The lapidary prose and especially the potent dose of humor evident throughout these essays are also vintage Panofsky—Panofsky in his American phase, be it noted, for neither of these things can be said of his earlier work in German.[33] Concerning the first point, Panofsky himself described the transformation toward economy of thought and expression entailed by his adjustment to the English language used in his adopted country.[34] What he did not mention is an equally profound transformation of his academic persona. Panofsky's wit had always been irrepressible and legendary, from cradle to grave, as it were; witness the immortal epitaph that he said came to him in a dream after spending an afternoon with his granddaughter:

> *He hated babies, gardening, and birds;*
> *But loved a few adults, all dogs, and words.*[35]

I speak here of the infusion of this personal quality into the normally solemn koine of scholarly discourse. The charm and humor that abound in almost everything he wrote in English were a product of his Americanization. They were his own invention, however, for they were no more native to previous American scholarship in art history than they were to European. And they brought a breath of fresh air to academe, both here and abroad.

Introduction

I

What Is Baroque?

Erwin Panofsky

The late-Scholastic logicians devised amusing helps to memory by which the many forms or figures of syllogism (conclusions from a major and minor premise) could be remembered. These mnemonic devices consisted of words of three syllables partly real and partly made up for the purpose. Each syllable stood for one of the three propositions, and the vowels therein signified the character of these propositions. The vowel *a*, for instance, denoted a general and positive statement; the vowel *o*, a partial and negative one. Thus the nice name *Barbara*, with its three *a*s, designates a syllogism that consists of three general and positive propositions (for instance: "All men are mortal—all mortal beings need food—consequently all men need food"). And for a syllogism consisting of one general and positive proposition and two partial and negative ones (for instance: "All cats have whiskers—some animals have no whiskers—consequently some animals are not cats"), there was coined the word *Baroco*, containing one *a* and two *o*s. Either the word, or the peculiarly roundabout fashion of the train of thought denoted by it, or both, must have struck later generations as particularly funny and characteristic of the pedantic formalism to which they objected in medieval thought; and when humanistic writers, including Montaigne, wished to ridicule an unworldly and sterile pedant, they reproached him with having his head full of "Barbara and Baroco," etc. Thus it came about that the word *Baroco* (French and English *Baroque*) came to signify everything wildly abstruse, obscure, fanciful, and useless (much as the word *intellectual* in many circles today). (The other derivation of the term from Latin *veruca* and Spanish *barueca*, meaning, originally, a wart and by extension a pearl of irregular shape, is most improbable both for logical and purely linguistic reasons.)[1]

The classicism of the eighteenth century applied this derogatory term especially to the type of architecture and ornament of which it disapproved, with special reference to the style of the great seventeenth-century architect Francesco Borromini. But in the nineteenth century, when Ranke

---

The reader should bear in mind that the text here reproduced is the typescript of a lecture (version 4, see pp. 202–3, note 13), not carefully edited by the author and interspersed with occasionally telegraphic asides and sometimes indecipherable handwritten notes, corrections, and slide indications (to which the illustrations correspond). I have made a few minor emendations to ensure intelligibility, and provided a few explanatory notes. In some cases the commonly accepted attributions of works of art have changed, and I have given the modern identifications.—Ed.

said "every period is immediately under God," this originally derogatory term—like the terms *Gothic* and *Rococo*—came to be divested of its vituperative connotations and was converted into a *neutral* designation, denoting "the style that followed the Renaissance"—that is to say, the style of the seventeenth and early-eighteenth centuries. This neutralization or, if you prefer, historicization of the old term of opprobrium led to several *extensions* of its use, some of which have their dangers, too. First of all, we have the harmless extension as to media within the visual arts: what had originally been limited to architecture and ornament was (again, by the way, just like "Gothic" and "Rococo") applied to sculpture and painting. Second, we have the less harmless extension as to media *outside* the visual arts (but still within the period), so that we now speak of Baroque poetry, music, and even mathematics. Third, we have the still less harmless extension *beyond* the period, so that every style supposedly related to a preceding one as "Baroque," properly speaking, is supposed to be related to the Renaissance, can be denoted by such composite appellations as "Hellenistic Baroque," "Romanesque Baroque," "Late Gothic Baroque," etc.

All this has resulted in considerable confusion; and this confusion is aggravated by the fact that the term *Baroque*, in its neutralized form doubtless the property of *art* historians, was and is applied by non–art historians who cannot always keep step with the gradual correction of the art historians' own errors. Even today, non–art historians and even a few misguided characters among the art historians themselves apply the term *Baroque* indiscriminately to Bernini and Tintoretto, Rubens, and El Greco because the book that seems to be accepted as a kind of Bible by the non–art historian, Wölfflin's "Principles of Art History," conceives of Baroque as a diametrical opposite to the so-called classic Renaissance. Wölfflin himself did not commit the sin of commission to call Tintoretto or El Greco "Baroque," but he committed the sin of omission not to include them—and what they stood for—in his considerations at all. His book does not mention a single work of art executed between, roughly speaking, the death of Raphael in 1520 and the full-fledged seventeenth century. And when we thus simply eliminate what happened in the hundred years in between, we do receive the impression of a straight, diametrical contrast between Baroque and Renaissance where, in reality, a much more complex development had taken place.[2]

The first idea that comes to our mind when the word *Baroque* is heard is the idea of a lordly racket, so to speak: unbridled movement, over-

fig. 1. Bernini, *Cathedra Petri.* Rome, St. Peter's (photo: Anderson 197).

fig. 2. Andrea Sansovino, tomb of Cardinal Ascanio Sforza. Rome, S. Maria del Popolo
(photo: Alinari 6156).

whelming richness in color and composition, theatrical effects produced by a free play of light and shade, and indiscriminate mixture of materials and techniques, and so forth. It is perfectly true that a work such as Bernini's *Cathedra Petri* (fig. 1) shows all these qualities in the highest degree. Sculptures of bronze, marble, and stucco merge with each other and with the architecture of the choir into one almost visionary spectacle, and not only the borderline between the various units and media, but also the borderline between art and nature is thoroughly obliterated (rays of natural light coming through the stained-glass window seem to continue in bronze beams, and the natural clouds seem to have condensed into plastic ones).[3]

Thus Bernini's *Cathedra* appears in fact as a diametrical opposite to a High Renaissance work such as Andrea Sansovino's tomb of Cardinal Ascanio Sforza (fig. 2; 1505–6); here we have a perfectly self-sufficient structure, consisting of a clear, flawlessly architectonic framework that keeps apart from the architecture of the church and provides "living rooms"—in the literal sense of the word—for the sculptures so that every figure exists and moves in its own compartment with self-sufficiency and freedom.

But we must bear in mind that a work like the *Cathedra Petri* (finished in 1661) represents a culminating phase of the Baroque development that marks a new and final step within the period as a whole. To understand the original direction of this development, we must compare it with what had immediately preceded it. What had immediately preceded it, and what is entirely eliminated from the calculations of Wölfflin and his followers, is a style that does include such phenomena as Tintoretto and El Greco—the style now generally referred to as mannerism (also, of course, originally a depreciatory term used by the seventeenth-century critics against late-sixteenth-century art much as the term *Baroque* was used by the eighteenth-century critics against seventeenth-century art). When we juxtapose Baroque art with pictures or sculptures executed by these mannerists, we cannot help realizing that the Baroque phenomenon amounted, at its inception, to a reaction against exaggeration and overcomplication, and that is due to a new tendency towards clarity, natural simplicity, and even equilibrium.

Giorgio Vasari's *Immaculate Conception* (fig. 3) shows a complicated two-dimensional pattern without spatial economy, yet very plastic modeling of the individual units. A kind of unresolved and even unresolvable tension makes itself felt in the distorted proportions and twisted movements of the

fig. 3. Giorgio Vasari, *Allegory of the Immaculate Conception.* Florence, Ss. Apostoli
(photo: Alinari 31036).

figures. This applies also to the subject matter, a very complicated allegory of the salvation of mankind by the Immaculate Conception of the Virgin.

Compared with this, a Baroque interpretation of a comparable subject (fig. 4) appears almost akin to a Madonna of Raphael. There is, it is true, a pictorial breadth, a highly emotional character and a vivacious mixture of reality and imagination that we would never encounter in a High Renaissance composition, but the Baroque picture is certainly less constrained and more balanced in space than the Vasari altarpiece and free from those convulsive entanglements that were characteristic of mannerism. The subject, too, is simply human, or humanly simple, understandable without a learned commentary.

Thus the Baroque appears primarily as a liquidation of that mannerism to which Tintoretto and El Greco really belong; but mannerism, in turn, was far from being the result of a mere whim of some oversophisticated artists: it was the expression of a real problem, inherent in Renaissance art from the outset.

The Renaissance movement itself, based as it was on both a classical revival and a quite nonclassical naturalism, and enforcing these tendencies within the limits of an essentially Christian civilization, had given rise to a style that, with all its merits, reveals a certain interior discrepancy. In early Renaissance pictures such as Ghirlandaio's *Adoration of the Shepherds* (fig. 5; 1485), the conflicting qualities are not as yet fully reconciled and are therefore easily discernible. The picture teems with archaeology, so to speak; it exhibits a classical sarcophagus, classical pillars and capitals, and even a triumphal arch in the background; but the animals and the shepherds are taken over from a Flemish altarpiece that appealed strongly to the realistic tendencies of the period (the famous Portinari altarpiece by Hugo van der Goes, imported into Florence some years before; fig. 6). The master has a satisfactory command of perspective, the typical Renaissance method of suggesting three-dimensional space, but this spatial tendency is counteracted by the persistence of a Gothic spirit that makes the figures cling to the frontal plane and to each other, so that the landscape appears as a backdrop rather than as a comprehensive three-dimensional medium. Thus the Renaissance style is characterized by interior contradictions practically unknown to the Middle Ages. The High Renaissance style of Leonardo and Raphael is a wonderful

fig. 4. Pietro da Cortona, *Virgin Appearing to St. Francis.* Rome, Vatican Museum.

fig. 5. Ghirlandaio, *Adoration of the Shepherds.* Florence, S. Trìnita (photo: Alinari 1412).

fig. 6. Hugo van der Goes, Portinari altarpiece. Florence, Uffizi (photo: Alinari 58209).

reconciliation of these contradictory tendencies. In a picture such as Raphael's *Madonna di Foligno* (fig. 7; ca. 1513), pagan beauty and Christian spirituality, a well-balanced two-dimensional pattern and an equilibrated distribution of plastic bodies in three-dimensional space, the plastic value of the figures and the pictorial values of the landscape—all this is fused into a truly classic unity. But we can easily foresee that this reconciliation could not last. No sooner had it been achieved in Rome than it was opposed by an anticlassic tendency that first developed in Tuscany, where the Quattrocento tradition and even Gothic spirit had persisted, and came to the surface as an almost violent reaction against the classic harmony (Pontormo, Rosso in Florence, Beccafumi in Siena, Parmigianino in North Italy, the first generation of mannerists).

In Pontormo's murals in the Certosa di Val d'Ema (fig. 8), 1522–23, we have almost no perspective at all, and in addition the plastic forms are dissolved by means of a curiously loose, oscillating technique. The movements do not show the classic contrápposto, but either shrill contrasts or rigid stiffness; the proportions are elongated in a deliberately unnatural way. The whole composition is compressed into a seemingly unearthly network of figures. It is a revival of preclassic tendencies, and it is not by accident that these frescoes are strongly influenced by northern art (Dürer), although even Dürer appears almost classic and harmonious when compared with his Italian follower (fig. 9). This new style means certainly both an enormous increase of spiritual intensity and emotional expression, and an enormous loss of harmony.

What applies to these frescoes by Pontormo applies also to the *Descent of Christ into Limbo*, executed about 1528 by the Sienese painter Beccafumi (fig. 10). In it can be seen a similar increase of intensity and a similar tendency towards pictorial dissolution at the expense of equilibrium, clarity, and plastic compactness, and this picture, too, is strongly influenced by a woodcut of Dürer (fig. 11).

It is interesting to compare Beccafumi's *Descent of Christ into Limbo* with a representation of the same subject executed about 1552, that is, about twenty-five years later (fig. 12). It illustrates the second phase of the manneristic style, a phase already known to us by Vasari's altarpiece, dominated by the influence of the Florentine phase of Michelangelo. This picture is by Bronzino, and is a typical representation of this second phase of mannerism.

fig. 7. Raphael, *Madonna di Foligno.* Rome, Vatican Museum (photo: Alinari 7722).

fig. 8. Pontormo, *Resurrection*. Florence, Certosa di Galluzzo (photo: Alinari 45993).

fig. 9. Dürer, *Resurrection*, woodcut.

fig. 10.   Beccafumi, *Descent into Limbo.* Siena, Pinacoteca Nazionale (photo: Anderson 21059).

fig. 11. Dürer, *Descent into Limbo,* woodcut.

fig. 12. Bronzino, *Descent into Limbo.* Florence, Museo di Santa Croce (photo: Alinari 456).

It is indubitably based on Beccafumi's composition; but for this very reason the changes are all the more evident. We observe a new systematization, a new firmness of outline, and a new emphasis on plastic values; but these plastic tendencies struggle so much the more against the tendency to compress the composition into an overcomplicated two-dimensional pattern, almost suppressing every spatial value. It is a consolidation, but a consolidation even more obstructive to classic harmony than had been the dissolution of Pontormo and Beccafumi. The style goes frozen, crystalline, with an enamel-like smoothness and hardness. The movements assume an overgraceful and at the same time constrained and bashful character. The whole of the composition becomes a battlefield of contradictory forces, entangled in an everlasting tension.

This second phase of the mannerist style lingered until the very end of the sixteenth century and even further. But in Italy, there set in about 1590 the countermovement that was to lead to what we call Baroque; and here we must remember one thing that, if forgotten, also leads to considerable confusion, namely that Baroque—like Renaissance—is an *Italian* phenomenon, and that the other European countries, which had all remained Gothic, to some extent at least, beneath the veneer of the imported Renaissance, thus tended to remain mannerist, to some extent at least, within the framework of the Baroque; it is this Baroque in partibus infidelium that fits the customary categories of wildness, obscurity, etc., much better and much more consistently than does the original, Italian version of the style.

In Italy, and in its earlier phases, Baroque means indeed a revolt against mannerism rather than against the "classic" Renaissance. It means, in fact, a deliberate reinstatement of classic principles and, at the same time, a reversion to nature, both stylistically and emotionally. In painting we can distinguish between two main forces that brought about this twofold change: the revolutionary effort of Caravaggio, who even by his contemporaries was called a "naturalist"; and the reformatory endeavor of the Bolognese Carracci school, which, like Ludovico Cigoli in Florence, tried to overcome the manneristic tendencies by obviously and purposely restoring the "good old traditions," so to speak. These two trends are in reality not irreconcilable opposites, but may be compared to the right and left wings of the phalanx, and in fact the further development is based on both, although it is true that the starting point of Caravaggio on the one hand and of the Carracci on the other was really different.

fig. 13. Caravaggio, *Still Life with Basket of Fruit*. Milan, Galleria Ambrosiana
(photo: Anderson 19535).

Caravaggio wanted to get rid of the worn-out formulae of the mannerists. He began with still-life painting (fig. 13) and gradually proceeded to rendering human figures of a realistic character. He shattered the artificial world of mannerism to build a new one out of its very elements: solid, three-dimensional bodies and light (chiaroscuro, first purely plastic, later spatial). He went into the quarry, so to speak, to get the blocks for a new structure entirely his own; but in putting these blocks together (so as to weave a coherent composition out of his realistic units) even he had to resume, to some extent, the devices of early sixteenth-century art: we can recognize in his pictures reminiscences of such High Renaissance masters as Lotto, Michelangelo, and even Raphael and the Antique (fig. 14).

Annibale Carracci, on the other hand, began with a deliberate effort to synthesize the plastic values of classical antiquity and classic High Renaissance art with such purely pictorial tendencies as had survived the manneristic intermezzo, namely the Venetian colorism and the Correggesque "sfumato." A picture like his *Sleeping Venus* (fig. 15), inspired as it is by Titian on the one hand (fig. 16) and classical statuary (fig. 17) on the other, is certainly a little cool and academic in style, though admirable in its wonderful composure and in its combination of sheer design with the coloristic richness and a fine silvery tonality in the landscape.

A later work by the same master, the *Lamentation* (fig. 18), already announces the general loosening of the style and the new emotionality characteristic of the high Baroque attitude. The mourning figures seem already to revel in their own sorrow, a new decisive factor in the Baroque psychology, and all the elements are interwoven into a luminous unity. The intrinsic dualism of postmedieval art, clearly discernible in the Ghirlandaio, admirably reconciled or perhaps only concealed in Raphael and other classic masters, and sharpened to a painful interior tension in the manneristic period, still subsists in a "Baroque" picture like this. But it is no longer a smoldering tension as in mannerism, but the conflicts and contrasts between plastic and spatial tendencies, ideal beauty and reality, neopagan humanism and Christian spiritualism, while still subsisting, begin to merge into a new sphere of highly subjective sensations, which manifest themselves in such subjective values as the picturesque play of light and shadow; the deep though definitely irrational space, and the soft, melting facial expressions. The Baroque attitude can be defined as being based on an objective conflict between antagonistic forces, which, however, merge into a subjective feeling of freedom and

fig. 14.   Caravaggio, *Bacchus*. Florence, Uffizi (photo: Alinari 46234).

fig. 15. Annibale Carracci, *Sleeping Venus*. Chantilly, Musée Condé (photo: Giraudon PE7298).

fig. 16. Titian, *Bacchanal of the Andrians*. Madrid, Prado (photo: Anderson 16365).

fig. 17. *Ariadne.* Rome, Vatican Museum (photo: Alinari 27011).

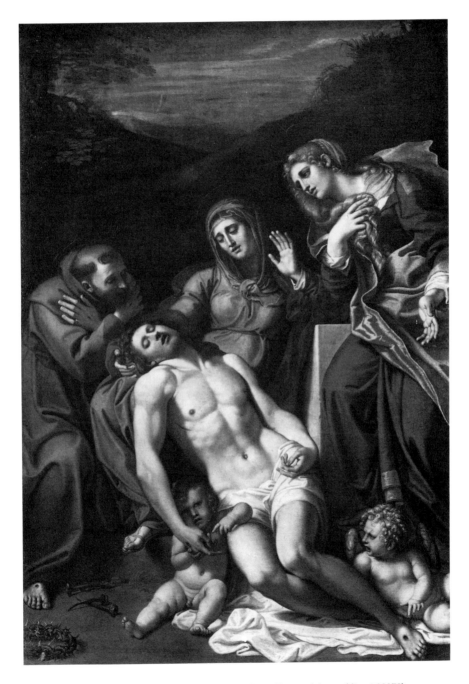

fig. 18. Annibale Carracci, *Lamentation.* Paris, Louvre (photo: Alinari 23078).

fig. 19.   Michelangelo, entrance-hall to the Laurentian Library. Florence, San Lorenzo
(photo: Alinari 1905).

even pleasure: the paradise of the High Renaissance regained after the struggles and tensions of the manneristic period, though still haunted (and enlivened) by the intense consciousness of an underlying dualism.

Thus the Baroque gave rise to a type of architecture in which the conflict between the wall and the structural members—a conflict introduced but cleverly harmonized in Renaissance architecture—no longer fills the beholder with a feeling of either cancerous disintegration as is the case in ordinary manneristic architecture, or stifling oppression, as is the case with Michelangelo's personal interpretation of mannerism (entrance-hall to the Laurentian Library, with its painfully incarcerated columns; fig. 19). For Baroque architecture breaks up, or even curves, the walls, so as to express a free dynamic interaction between mass and the energies of the structural members, and to display a quasi-theatrical scenery that integrates the conflicting elements into a spatial ensemble, enlivened by chiaroscuro values and even indicating a kind of osmotic interrelation between exterior and interior space (figs. 20, 21).

Similarly Baroque art gave up the principle of manneristic sculpture of driving the spectator around the groups and figures by a rotating composition, without ever allowing him to acquiesce in one predominating view (fig. 22). "A good sculpture must have a hundred views," says Benvenuto Cellini (and this is one of the major tenets of manneristic sculpture) in contradiction to Leonardo da Vinci who, as a true High Renaissance artist, had been of the opinion that a sculpture worked in the round was nothing but a combination of two reliefs, one displaying the figure in front view, the other from the back. Baroque statues and groups neither deny the conflict between a two-dimensional "view" and three-dimensional bodies, nor do they use this conflict to fill the beholder with a feeling of restlessness and dissatisfaction: they revert to the one-view principle (fig. 23), but this one view is no longer achieved by disciplining the composition to a kind of relief arrangement, but includes so many torsions, foreshortenings, and spatial values (intervals between the various plastic units) that the "one-view" assumes the character of an imaginary picture plane on which are projected both plastic and spatial elements.[4] In point of fact, Baroque art liked to place sculptures in a picturesque or even stagelike setting (fig. 24).

Thus we can easily conceive that Baroque art came to abolish the borderline between the "three arts," and even between art and nature, and

fig. 20.   Borromini, S. Ivo della Sapienza, view of the cupola. Rome (photo: Anderson 27216).

fig. 21. Borromini, S. Ivo della Sapienza, view in the cupola. Rome (photo: Alinari 49134).

fig. 22.   Giambologna, *Rape of the Sabines.* Florence, Loggia dei Lanzi
(photo: Alinari 2502).

fig. 23. Bernini, *St. Longinus.* Rome, St. Peter's (photo: Anderson 20588).

fig. 24. Bernini, tomb of Alexander VII. Rome, St. Peter's (photo: Anderson 198).

also brought forth the modern landscape in the full sense of the word (fig. 25), meaning a visualization of unlimited space captured in, and represented by, a section of it, so that human figures became debased to a mere "staffage" and finally could be dispensed with altogether. In the North (fig. 26; this Van Goyen is a comparatively moderate specimen), even the quasi-architectonic features of the scenery itself could be subdued or suppressed in favor of extensions as such, the picture showing nothing but the endless horizontal plain or ocean, and the sky occupying four-fifths or five-sixths of the area of the picture. In all these cases a tension between the two-dimensional surface and three-dimensional space is utilized as a means of subjective intensification. This is a fundamental attitude of Baroque art. A conflict of antagonistic forces merging into a subjective unity, and thus resolved, is also, or rather most particularly, to be observed in the realm of psychology. While in Annibale Carracci's *Lamentation* sorrow becomes so strong that it almost transforms itself into pleasure, in the same way the unutterable bliss of a heavenly apparition—now within reach of a mortal being—can become so strong that it begins to hurt, which makes the pleasure all the more intense. Thus we can understand the supreme incarnation of the Baroque spirit, the *Ecstasy of St. Theresa* by Bernini, in S. Maria della Vittoria in Rome (figs. 27, 28). In this work, again a half plastic group, half relief, half picture, the pain of the golden arrow piercing the heart of the saint actually fuses with the supreme happiness of her union with Christ, so that the spiritual bliss could melt with the spasms of a quasi-erotic ecstasy. This experience, characteristic as it is of the attitude of many mystics, has often been described in religious literature (particularly by St. Theresa herself), but it took the Baroque style to express it in visual form.

The very physiognomy of the human beings reflects the evolution that led from the classic High Renaissance to mannerism, and from mannerism to Baroque; and this physiognomical change is perhaps the most revealing symptom of the psychological processes that lie at the base of the stylistic phenomena.

Raphael, *Donna Velata* (fig. 29): pyramidal composition, principle of axiality. Perfect harmony also psychologically. Absolutely restricted to her own existence, regardless of the outer world but profoundly acquiescing in herself; a rounded-off microcosm, comparable to a star revolving around its own axis, symbolizing the short-lived equilibrium of the contradictory forces

fig. 25. Annibale Carracci, *Landscape with Hunting Scene*. Paris, Louvre.

fig. 26.   Jan Van Goyen, *View of the Rhein at Arnheim*. Vaduz, Liechtenstein Collection.

fig. 27. Bernini, *Ecstasy of St. Theresa.* Rome, S. Maria della Vittoria (photo: Alinari 6193).

fig. 28. Bernini, *Ecstasy of St. Theresa,* detail. Rome, S. Maria della Vittoria (photo: Alinari 6193.B).

fig. 29. Raphael, *Donna Velata*. Florence, Palazzo Pitti (photo: Alinari 130).

fig. 30.   Pontormo, *Study for the Deposition of Christ*. Florence, Uffizi (photo: Gundersheimer 7048).

fig. 31. Pontormo, *Portrait of a Young Boy.* Malibu, J. Paul Getty Museum.

in postmedieval civilization. This calm and self-sufficient attitude was shattered very soon.

Pontormo, *Study for the Deposition of Christ* (fig. 30): stirred, even frightened expression. The individual becomes aware of both the problems of the outer world and the problems of his or her own self, with the result that people shrink from the world as from a menacing danger. In fact, when this drawing was made, a crisis had broken out in the field of religion and thought, but people were not fully awake to the fact that it was a crisis, and felt only disturbed by a general atmosphere of restlessness and insecurity. It was felt, but not yet fully realized, that there was a discrepancy between beauty and virtue, morality and freedom, humanism and Christianity, faith and science. People were dissatisfied with the religious situation, but in Italy and even in Germany they did not yet know whether they were still faithful Catholics or heretics, and often had recourse to a kind of mysticism that differed from but was not opposed to the orthodox dogma. This unsettled and disturbed attitude is even discernible in Pontormo's *Portrait of a Young Boy* (fig. 31), and may be described as "open, but disharmonious," while the High Renaissance attitude (Raphael) can be described as "harmonious, but closed." And this applies to the formal values (composition, handling of the medium) as well as to the psychological interpretation.

A portrait attributed to Bronzino in the Frick Collection (fig. 32) is a characteristic specimen of the second phase of mannerism, which is the very style of the Counter Reformation. It sets in almost precisely with the beginning of the Council of Trent and outlasts it only by a few decades. Now things were settled, but freedom of life and thought, happiness, and even beauty had to be sacrificed on the altar of the dogma, now firmly reestablished but oppressive and tyrannical as long as its rule was still threatened—and the same was true of morals and customs (Spanish dress; Tasso).[5] Thus such a portrait has in common with the Raphael portrait that the figure is again quiet and full of composure; but it differs from it in that carriage and expression are emphatically uneasy and unhappy. While in the Raphael portraits the self-restriction revealed a complete freedom and self-sufficient harmony, it reveals here a constrained reserve deliberately secluding itself from the outer world. It is as though the life of these people had gone frozen, or hides itself behind a motionless mask, melancholy and cool, shy and supercilious at the same time.

fig. 32. Bronzino, *Ludovico Capponi*. New York, Frick Collection.

The twisted and constrained mentality of the Counter Reformation period shows in innumerable phenomena: for instance, in the frightful conflicts between religious dogma and scientific thought (a problem that had not existed for a man like Leonardo da Vinci), but the most illuminating fact is perhaps the reaction of the period upon the beautiful nude in general and the classical nude in particular. Invectives were hurled against Michelangelo's *Last Judgement* (fig. 33), which escaped destruction only by a thorough chastening.[6] The church stated that classical marbles could be tolerated only if they were not exposed to public view; the sculptor Ammannati (at the age of seventy-one, it is true) repented in sackcloth and ashes for having made figures so scantily dressed, and the bronze fig leaf affixed to classical statues is a very characteristic invention of this period. On the other hand, both artist and art lovers were in reality no less susceptible to the beauty of classical nudes than were the Renaissance people, only their enthusiasm was marred—and sharpened—by a guilty conscience. What in the days of Raphael had been a matter of course now become a matter of either cool archaeological interest or sinful excitement, and often a mixture of both.

In Bronzino's *Descent into Limbo* (fig. 12), the Eve is a literal adaptation of the Venus of Knidos (fig. 34), much more archaeological than in any work of Raphael; but just this combination of classic beauty with a bashful posture and a seeming intangibility makes the figure almost ambiguous. The beholder feels that beauty is looked upon as something dangerous or even prohibited, and for this very reason is struck by these frozen crystalline nudes as by something more voluptuous and intoxicating than the straightforwardness of High Renaissance art or the sensual brio of the Baroque.

It is therefore not by accident that the Rococo or Louis XV style of the eighteenth century, striving for emotional values of a more or less lascivious kind, shows often an unmistakable similarity to the later phase of mannerism. The *Amor and Psyche* by Jacopo Zucchi (fig. 35), a pupil of Vasari, in the Borghese Gallery (1589) strikes us as an actual anticipation of Charles Joseph Natoire's representation of the same scene in the decoration of the Hôtel de Soubise (fig. 36), completed exactly 150 years later, in 1739.[7] Thus, the proud and melancholy remoteness of mannerist portraits eloquently expresses the interior tensions or "inhibitions" of the Counter Reformation period, whether we consider a young man such as the *Ludovico Capponi* (fig. 32) in the Frick Collection, or a great lady such as *Eleanora of Toledo, Grandduchess of Tuscany,* as portrayed by Bronzino (fig. 37).

fig. 33. Michelangelo, *Last Judgement.* Rome, Vatican, Sistine Chapel (photo: Anderson 933).

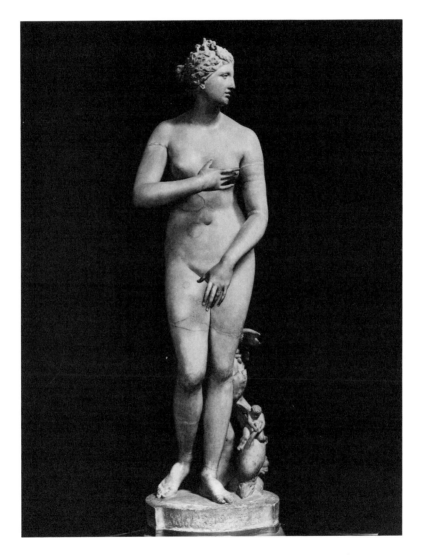

fig. 34. Venus of Knidos. Florence, Uffizi (photo: Alinari 1332).

fig. 35. Jacopo Zucchi, *Amor and Psyche*. Rome, Galleria Borghese (photo: Anderson 4806).

fig. 36. Charles Joseph Natoire, *Amor and Psyche*. Paris, Hôtel de Soubise (photo: Marburg, 48 942).

fig. 37. Bronzino, *Eleanora of Toledo, Grandduchess of Tuscany.* Berlin, Staatliche Museen.

A Baroque portrait, however, is free and open to the world again. The attitude of Bernini's *Costanza Buonarelli* (fig. 38) is sensuously cheerful, throbbing with unrepressed vitality, harmonious in spite of her susceptibility to every kind of impression and emotion. The Baroque (I am speaking only of Italy, where the style originated) had overcome the crisis of the Counter Reformation. A modus vivendi had been found in every field; scientists were no longer burnt like Giordano Bruno (whose death might be called an emphatically manneristic occurrence, while the release of Campanella by Urban VIII was a Baroque event); Roman sculptures were no longer hidden in cellars; the system of the church was now so powerful and undisputed that it could afford to be comparatively tolerant towards any vital effort, and more than that: it would gradually assimilate and absorb these vital forces, and finally allow the very churches to be filled with that visual symphony of gay putti, glittering gold and theatrical sceneries as seen in the *Cathedra Petri*. In the field of portraits this gorgeous decoration has a parallel in that late bust by Bernini of *Louis XVI* (fig. 39), the triumphal outburst of the new freedom gradually conquered during the seventeenth century.

The release or deliverance achieved by the Baroque period can be observed in every field of human endeavor. The Florentine intermedios of the manneristic theater (similar to the English masks) abounded in such complicated allegories as seen in the Intermedio of 1585 and 1589 where the conclusion of Plato's *Republic* appeared on the stage, including the Planets, the Harmony of the Spheres, the Three Goddesses of Fate, and even Necessity, holding the adamantine axis of the Universe (fig. 40). We happen to possess the diary of a nobleman who saw this play and stated that it was very beautiful but nobody could understand what it was all about. A few years later these allegories were replaced by the modern opera, full of natural emotions and tuneful melodies (Rinuccini's *Daphne*, 1594; Monteverdi's *Orpheus*, a bit later). The very style of writing had assumed a specific manneristic character all over the continent (Gongorism in Spain, Euphuism in England: Lyly, Green, and Donne). This too was overcome by Cervantes and Shakespeare. A beautiful instance is Shakespeare's *Winter's Tale* (1610–11) deliberately ridiculing the euphuistic prose of the courtiers, and opposing to it the emotional and even versified, but beautifully natural, profoundly human speech of the main characters,

> *Courtier:* One of the prettiest touches of all . . . was when, at the relation
> of the Queen's death (with the manner how she came to it

bravely confessed and lamented by the king) how attentiveness
wounded his daughter, till, from one sign of dolor to another, she
did, with an 'Alas,' I would fain say, bleed tears; for, I am sure my
heart wept blood. Who was most marble, there changed color;
some swooned, all sorrowed.
(*The Winter's Tale* 5.2.80–89)

Perdita:　And do not say 'tis superstition, that I kneel, and then implore
her blessing. . . . Lady, Dear Queen, that ended when I but
began, Give me that hand of yours to kiss.
(*The Winter's Tale* 5.3.44–47),

and with a significant change in the story as compared to Shakespeare's
model, Robert Greene's *Pandosto* of 1588. This kind of "happy end" is a typical Baroque feature (in Monteverdi's opera even Orpheus remains in possession of his wife): a painful conflict resolved in a pleasurable issue. (Compare
the very anecdotes about Bernini's busts of Scipione Borghese and the Fon-
tana dei Quattro Fiumi.[8])

In the plastic arts, the increase of emotional values resulting from a
conflict of opposite impulses, which still merge into one overwhelming feeling of subjective excitement, was already observed in such works as the *Virgin
Appearing to St. Francis* by Pietro da Cortona (fig. 4), or Bernini's *Ecstasy of
St. Theresa* (figs. 27, 28). But in addition, this tendency gave rise to the discovery of new iconographical subjects that conformed to the new trend of
imagination and feeling. The *Wounded St. Sebastian Nursed by the Pious Irene*
by Giovanni Domenico Cerrini (fig. 41): a new conception of martyr scenes,
physical pain intensely felt (in contrast with medieval and Renaissance representations) but fusing into a blissful rapture. In this case the saint is still fet-
tered to the tree, a drastic illustration of the conflict between physical pain
and relief. The episode is not entirely unknown in pre-Baroque art, but was
restricted to comprehensive series representing the whole life of Sebastian;
now the episode is singled out, emotionally intensified, and becomes a favorite subject of Baroque art. *Hagar Starving in the Desert, but Comforted by an
Angel* (fig. 42), Pier Francesco Mola (many other representations, e.g., Lan-
franco, Pietro da Cortona): the somewhat pathetic figure of Hagar, a favorite
character in Baroque art; also other incidents of her life (her return into
Abraham's house before the birth of Ishmael) and other scenes of reconciliation after a painful conflict (return of the prodigal son). On the other hand,
the triumphal feeling of *David after His Victory over Goliath* (Orazio Gen-

fig. 38. Bernini, *Costanza Buonarelli*. Florence, Bargello (photo: Alinari 2717).

fig. 39. Bernini, *Louis XIV.* Versailles (photo: Alinari 25588).

fig. 40.   Agostino Carracci after Bernardo Buontalenti, *The Harmony of the Spheres,* engraving.
First intermezzo for *La Pellegrina,* Florence, 1589.

fig. 41. Giovanni Domenico Cerrini, *Wounded St. Sebastian Nursed by Irene.* Rome, Galleria Colonna (photo: Anderson 20734).

fig. 42. Pier Francesco Mola, *Hagar Starving in the Desert but Comforted by an Angel.*
Rome, Galleria Colonna.

fig. 43. Orazio Gentileschi, *David after His Victory over Goliath*. Rome, Galleria Spada
(photo: Alinari 28919).

tileschi; fig. 43) can mingle with what seems to be a deep compassion for the life destroyed, so that the very scene of triumph becomes transformed into a scene of melancholy brooding over the transience of human life. The contrast between Life and Death plays a formidable role in Baroque iconography, and one of the most characteristic innovations of the period is what we can term the blissful death—that is to say, a scene in which the agony of the dying human being and the mourning of the survivors merge with a feeling of supreme release: for example, Bernini's *Ludovica Albertoni* (fig. 44), Domenichino's *Last Communion of St. Jerome* (fig. 45).

It is true that in representations like these there appears a feeling that is commonly known as sentimentality. And the fact that Baroque art has been so emphatically disapproved of for almost two centuries is largely due to the impression that the feeling of Baroque figures lacked genuineness and sincerity. The beholder seemed to feel that these figures displayed theatrical poses, that they reveled in their own sensations, that they "did not mean it," so to speak, whether they exhibit their half painful, half blissful raptures, like the St. Sebastians and St. Lawrences, or their patient devoutness, like the *Mary Magdalen* by Guido Reni (fig. 46).

Now it is true that the psychological attitude of the figures in Baroque art is less unbroken [sic; unspoken?] than that of the figures in Renaissance art, let alone medieval art. But it would be unjust to doubt the genuineness of their feelings. The feeling of Baroque people is (or at least can be in the works of great masters) perfectly genuine, only it does not fill the whole of their souls. They not only feel, but are also aware of their own feelings. While their hearts are quivering with emotion, their consciousness stands aloof and "knows." Many a beholder may not like that. Only we should not forget that this psychological rift is the logical consequence of the historical situation, and at the same time the very foundation of what we call the "modern" form of imagination and thought. The experience of so many conflicts and dualisms between emotion and reflection, lust and pain, devoutness and voluptuousness had led to a kind of awakening, and thus endowed the European mind with a new consciousness. Now consciousness means, as the Bible has it, the loss of innocence, but on the other hand the possibility of being "like God," that is to say, superior to one's own reactions and sensations. Sentimentality is only a negative aspect of this new consciousness (when the individual not only becomes aware of his or her feelings but also consciously indulges in them), and another negative aspect—and the logical

fig. 44. Bernini, *Ludovica Albertoni*. Rome, S. Francesco a Ripa (photo: Anderson 2385).

fig. 45.   Domenichino, *Last Communion of St. Jerome.* Rome, Vatican Museum (photo: Alinari 7752).

fig. 46. Guido Reni, *Mary Magdalen*. Baltimore, Walters Art Gallery.

fig. 47.   Adriaen Brouwer, *Classical Divinities.* Formerly private collection, now lost (from *Richard Hamann in Memoriam* [Schriften zur Kunstgeschichte, I], Berlin, 1963, 93, fig. 102).

correlative of sentimentality—is frivolity (when the individual becomes aware of his or her feelings but belittles or even disintegrates them with a skeptical smile). There is a touch of frivolity, already realized by the contemporaries, even in the angel of Bernini's *Ecstasy of St. Theresa* (fig. 28).

But while sentimentality and frivolity are negative aspects of the new consciousness, there are two emphatically positive ones. First, the new "critical" attitude and method of thinking as achieved by Descartes, for the famous *cogito, ergo sum* [I think, therefore I am] means no less than that the human mind no longer accepts any other premise than the consciousness of its own activity, and thus claims the right to build up a system of thought entirely independent of both brute matter of fact and dogmatic belief. It is quite interesting, though, that Descartes himself, for instance in a letter describing his situation in Amsterdam, could display both a slight frivolity and a slight sentimentality, both these elements transfigured by a wonderful reticence and self-irony.[9] This leads us to the second positive aspect of that new consciousness that is the curse and the bliss of the new psychology developing in the Baroque era: the sense of humor in the true sense of the term. For the sense of humor, as it appears in Shakespeare and Cervantes—not to be confounded with wit or mere comicality—is based on the fact that a man realizes that the world is not quite what it should be, but does not get angry about it, nor think that he himself is free from ugliness and from the major and minor vices and stupidities that he observes.

It is the satirist, not the humorist, who considers himself to be cleverer and better than other people. The humorist, thanks to that consciousness that keeps him at a distance from reality as well as from himself, is capable of both: of noticing the objective shortcomings of life and human nature—that is to say, the discrepancies between reality and ethical or aesthetic postulates—and of subjectively overcoming this discrepancy (therefore the sense of humor is really a Baroque quality) in that he understands it as the result of a universal, even metaphysical imperfection willed by the maker of the world. Thus the real humorist, in contrast with the satirist, not only excuses what he ridicules but deeply sympathizes with it; he even glorifies it, in a way, because he conceives it as a manifestation of the same power that shows itself in the things reputed to be grand and sublime, whereas they are, sub specie aeternitatis, just as far from perfection as the things reputed to be small and ridiculous.

fig. 48.   Leonardo da Vinci, *Grotesque Heads,* drawing. Windsor Castle.

fig. 49. Papal Donkey, woodcut.

fig. 50. *Monk-Calf,* woodcut.

This sense of humor that is creative rather than destructive, and requires an imaginative superiority and freedom by no means inferior to the intellectual superiority and freedom of a critical philosopher, shows not only in the poetry and literature of the Baroque period, but also in its plastic arts. We can enjoy it in the gigantic, quasi-aboriginal jokes of Adriaen Brouwer.

Classical Divinities by Adriaen Brouwer (fig. 47):[10] Mercury as an old salesman, Mars as the typical boasting soldier, Apollo as a village fiddler with a penny flute at his hat, Neptune carrying a huge over-rake. And in a more refined variety we find it in the first caricatures—that is to say, in pictorial criticisms of individuals that make us really laugh, because they ridicule an individual while revealing the limits of human nature as such. In this sense caricatures are really a Baroque invention (Carracci; the thing was so new that Bernini had to explain the very word to the French noblemen when he came to Paris).[11]

Leonardo's so-called caricatures are by no means meant to be funny (fig. 48). They register extremes, outstanding natural phenomena, and are far too dispassionate and too little individualized to make us laugh. They may fill us instead with a kind of horror and could be used, if for anything, to characterize the viciousness of the Jews in the Pilate scene, or of nasty old scholars in such representations as Christ among the Doctors. The same thing is true of those cruelly insulting and humorless pictures that were hurled at an adversary during the struggles of the German Reformation, such as the *Papal Donkey* or the *Monk-Calf* (figs. 49, 50).

The really funny and relieving effect of a caricature in the true sense of the word is based on the fact that the author keenly observes and even exaggerates the shortcomings of his victims, but still, or rather for this very reason, profoundly likes them as human beings created by God. Falstaff may be a liar and a coward and practically devoid of any capital virtue, but still he remains as likable a human being as Percy Hotspur (who is himself slightly caricatured), let alone the serious characters of the play. A parallel can be found in some delightful drawings by Bernini: bust of *Cardinal Scipione Borghese* (fig. 51), in which we note the half-closed button, a small but significant symptom of the fact that in the Baroque era dignity was compatible with nonchalance); caricature of the same illustrious person (fig. 52). Even the colossal vanity of a young *Captain of the Papal Guard* (fig. 53) could be glorified and transfigured, so to speak, in such a way that it becomes highly enjoyable, perhaps because we feel that the spirit of this captain is lurking in some

fig. 51. Bernini, *Cardinal Scipione Borghese*. Rome, Galleria Borghese (photo: Alinari 27468).

fig. 52. Bernini, *Caricature of Cardinal Scipione Borghese,* drawing. Rome, Vatican Library.

fig. 53. Bernini, *Captain of the Papal Guard,* drawing. Rome, Gabinetto Nazionale delle Stampe.

hidden corner of every human soul and may jump up unexpectedly as this Jack-in-the-box-like creature.

To sum up, the Baroque is not the decline, let alone the end of what we call the Renaissance era. It is in reality the second great climax of this period and, at the same time, the beginning of a fourth era, which may be called "Modern" with a capital M. It is the only phase of Renaissance civilization in which this civilization overcame its inherent conflicts not by just smoothing them away (as did the classic Cinquecento), but by realizing them consciously and transforming them into subjective emotional energy with all the consequences of this subjectivization. The Renaissance, when conceived as one of the three main epochs of human history—the others being antiquity and the Middle Ages—and when defined with Morey as the "period which had made man and nature more interesting than God," lasted much longer than until the end of the sixteenth century.[12] It lasted, roughly speaking, up to the time when Goethe died and the first railroads and industrial plants were built. For not until as late as that were man and nature (meaning man as a really human being and nature as the totality of natural things not tampered with by man) doomed to become less interesting and less important than those antihuman and antinatural forces that seem to determine our own period—the forces of masses and machines—and of which we don't yet know whether they are the manifestations of an unknown God or an unknown Devil. The rise of these new forces, not the Baroque movement, means the real end of the Renaissance, and at the same time the beginning of our own epoch of history, an epoch that is still struggling for an expression both in life and in art, and that will be named and judged by the generations to come—provided that it does not put an end to all generations to come.

II

Style and Medium in the Motion Pictures

Erwin Panofsky

Film art is the only art the development of which men now living have witnessed from the very beginnings; and this development is all the more interesting as it took place under conditions contrary to precedent. It was not an artistic urge that gave rise to the discovery and gradual perfection of a new technique; it was a technical invention that gave rise to the discovery and gradual perfection of a new art.

From this we understand two fundamental facts. First, that the primordial basis of the enjoyment of moving pictures was not an objective interest in a specific subject matter, much less an aesthetic interest in the formal presentation of subject matter, but the sheer delight in the fact that things seemed to move, no matter what things they were. Second, that films—first exhibited in "kinetoscopes," namely, cinematographic peep shows, but projectable to a screen since as early as 1894—are, originally, a product of genuine folk art (whereas, as a rule, folk art derives from what is known as "higher art"). At the very beginning of things we find the simple recording of movements: galloping horses, railroad trains, fire engines, sporting events, street scenes. And when it had come to the making of narrative films these were produced by photographers who were anything but "producers" or "directors," performed by people who were anything but actors, and enjoyed by people who would have been much offended had anyone called them "art lovers."

The casts of these archaic films were usually collected in a "café" where unemployed supers or ordinary citizens possessed of a suitable exterior were wont to assemble at a given hour. An enterprising photographer would walk in, hire four or five convenient characters, and make the picture while carefully instructing them what to do: "Now, you pretend to hit this lady over the head"; and (to the lady): "And you pretend to fall down in a heap." Productions like these were shown, together with those purely factual recordings of "movement for movement's sake," in a few small and dingy cinemas mostly frequented by the "lower classes" and a sprinkling of youngsters in quest of adventure (about 1905, I happen to remember, there was only one obscure and faintly disreputable *Kino* in the whole city of Berlin, bearing, for

---

Panofsky published this essay without illustrations; those included here are adopted from the edition by Campus Verlag mentioned in the preface.—Ed.

---

some unfathomable reason, the English name of "The Meeting Room"). Small wonder that the "better classes," when they slowly began to venture into these early picture theaters, did so, not by way of seeking normal and possibly serious entertainment, but with that characteristic sensation of self-conscious condescension with which we may plunge, in gay company, into the folkloristic depths of Coney Island or a European kermis; even a few years ago it was the regulation attitude of the socially or intellectually prominent that one could confess to enjoying such austerely educational films as *The Sex Life of the Starfish* or films with "beautiful scenery," but never to a serious liking for narratives.

Today there is no denying that narrative films are not only "art"— not often good art, to be sure, but this applies to other media as well—but also, besides architecture, cartooning, and "commercial design," the only visual art entirely alive. The "movies" have reestablished that dynamic contact between art production and art consumption which, for reasons too complex to be considered here, is sorely attenuated, if not entirely interrupted, in many other fields of artistic endeavor. Whether we like it or not, it is the movies that mold, more than any other single force, the opinions, the taste, the language, the dress, the behavior, and even the physical appearance of a public comprising more than 60 percent of the population of the earth. If all the serious lyrical poets, composers, painters, and sculptors were forced by law to stop their activities, a rather small fraction of the general public would become aware of the fact and a still smaller fraction would seriously regret it. If the same thing were to happen with the movies the social consequences would be catastrophic.

In the beginning, then, there were the straight recordings of movement no matter what moved, namely, the prehistoric ancestors of our "documentaries"; and, soon after, the early narratives, namely, the prehistoric ancestors of our "feature films." The craving for a narrative element could be satisfied only by borrowing from older arts, and one should expect that the natural thing would have been to borrow from the theater, a theater play being apparently the *genus proximum* to a narrative film in that it consists of a narrative enacted by persons that move. But in reality the imitation of stage performances was a comparatively late and thoroughly frustrated development. What happened at the start was a very different thing. Instead of imitating a theatrical performance already endowed with a certain amount of motion, the earliest films added movement to works of art originally stationary, so that the dazzling technical invention might achieve a triumph of its own without intruding upon the sphere of higher culture. The living language, which is always right, has endorsed this sensible choice when it still speaks of a "moving picture" or, simply, a "picture," instead of accepting the pretentious and fundamentally erroneous "screenplay."

The stationary works enlivened in the earliest movies were indeed pictures: bad nineteenth-century paintings and postcards (or waxworks à la Madame Tussaud's), supplemented by the comic strips—a most important root of cinematic art—and the subject matter of popular songs, pulp magazines, and dime novels; and the films descending from this ancestry appealed directly and very intensely to a folk art mentality. They gratified—often simultaneously—first, a primitive sense of justice and decorum when virtue and industry were rewarded while vice and laziness were punished; second, plain sentimentality when "the thin trickle of a fictive love interest" took its course "through somewhat serpentine channels," or when Father, dear Father returned from the saloon to find his child dying of diphtheria; third, a primordial instinct for bloodshed and cruelty when Andreas Hofer faced the firing squad, or when (in a film of 1893–94) the head of Mary Queen of Scots actually came off; fourth, a taste for mild pornography (I remember with great pleasure a French film of ca. 1900 wherein a seemingly but not really well-rounded lady as well as a seemingly but not really slender one were shown changing to bathing suits—an honest, straightforward *porcheria* much less objectionable than the now extinct Betty Boop films and, I am sorry to say, some of the more recent Walt Disney productions); and, finally, that crude sense of humor, graphically described as "slapstick," which feeds upon the sadistic and the pornographic instinct, either singly or in combination.

Not until as late as ca. 1905 was a film adaptation of *Faust* ventured upon (cast still "unknown," characteristically enough), and not until 1911 did Sarah Bernhardt lend her prestige to an unbelievably funny film tragedy, *Queen Elizabeth of England.* These films represent the first conscious attempt at transplanting the movies from the folk art level to that of "real art"; but they also bear witness to the fact that this commendable goal could not be reached in so simple a manner. It was soon realized that the imitation of a theater performance with a set stage, fixed entries and exits, and distinctly literary ambitions is the one thing the film must avoid.

The legitimate paths of evolution were opened, not by running away from the folk art character of the primitive film but by developing it within the limits of its own possibilities. Those primordial archetypes of film productions on the folk art level—success or retribution, sentiment, sensation, pornography, and crude humor—could blossom forth into genuine history, tragedy and romance, crime and adventure, and comedy, as soon as it was realized that they could be transfigured—not by an artificial injection of literary values but by the exploitation of the unique and specific possibilities of the new medium. Significantly, the beginnings of this legitimate development antedate the attempts at endowing the film with higher values of a foreign order (the crucial period being the years from 1902 to ca. 1905), and the decisive steps were taken by people who were laymen or outsiders from the viewpoint of the serious stage.

These unique and specific possibilities can be defined as *dynamization of space* and, accordingly, *spatialization of time.* This statement is self-evident to the point of triviality but it belongs to that kind of truth which, just because of its triviality, is easily forgotten or neglected.

In a theater, space is static, that is, the space represented on the stage, as well as the spatial relation of the beholder to the spectacle, is unalterably fixed. The spectator cannot leave his seat, and the setting of the stage cannot change, during one act (except for such incidentals as rising moons or gathering clouds and such illegitimate reborrowings from the film as turning wings or gliding backdrops). But, in return for this restriction, the theater has the advantage that time, the medium of emotion and thought conveyable by speech, is free and independent of anything that may happen in visible space. Hamlet may deliver his famous monologue lying on a couch in the middle distance, doing nothing and only dimly discernible to the spectator and listener, and yet by his mere words enthrall him with a feeling of intensest emotional action.

With the movies the situation is reversed. Here, too, the spectator occupies a fixed seat, but only physically, not as the subject of an aesthetic experience. Aesthetically, he is in permanent motion as his eye identifies itself with the lens of the camera, which permanently shifts in distance and direction. And as movable as the spectator is, as movable is, for the same reason, the space presented to him. Not only bodies move in space, but space itself does, approaching, receding, turning, dissolving and recrystallizing as it ap-

fig. 1.   The Story of Louis Pasteur. Frankfurt/Main, Deutsches Institut für Filmkunde.

pears through the controlled locomotion and focusing of the camera and through the cutting and editing of the various hosts—not to mention such special effects as visions, transformations, disappearances, slow-motion and fast-motion shots, reversals, and trick films. This opens up a world of possibilities of which the stage can never dream. Quite apart from such photographic tricks as the participation of disembodied spirits in the action of the *Topper* series,* or the more effective wonders wrought by Roland Young in *The Man Who Could Work Miracles*,† there is, on the purely factual level, an untold wealth of themes as inaccessible to the "legitimate" stage as a fog or snowstorm is to the sculptor; all sorts of violent elemental phenomena and, conversely, events too microscopic to be visible under normal conditions (such as the life-saving injection with the serum flown in at the very last moment, or the fatal bite of the yellow-fever mosquito); full-scale battle scenes; all kinds of operations, not only in the surgical sense but also in the sense of any actual construction, destruction, or experimentation, as in *Louis Pasteur*‡ (fig. 1) or *Madame Curie*;§ a really grand party, moving through many rooms of a mansion or a palace. Features like these, even the mere shifting of the scene from one place to another by means of a car perilously negotiating heavy traffic or a motorboat steered through a nocturnal harbor, will not only always retain their primitive cinematic appeal but also remain enormously effective as a means of stirring the emotions and creating suspense. In addition, the movies have the power, entirely denied to the theater, to convey psychological experiences by directly projecting their content to the screen, substituting, as it were, the eye of the beholder for the consciousness of the character (as when the imaginings and hallucinations of the drunkard in the otherwise overrated *Lost Weekend* [fig. 2] appear as stark realities instead of being described by mere words). But any attempt to convey thought and feelings exclusively, or even primarily, by speech leaves us with a feeling of embarrassment, boredom, or both.

Topper, 1937 (MGM), *Topper Takes a Trip,* 1939 (Hal Roach/United Artists), *Topper Returns,* 1941 (United Artists), all directed by Norman Z. McLeod, title role Roland Young. —Ed., as also following notes with symbols.

†*The Man Who Could Work Miracles,* England 1937, directed by Lothar Mendes, with Roland Young.

‡*The Story of Louis Pasteur,* 1935, directed by William Dieterle (Warner Bros.), with Paul Muni; *Madame Curie,* 1943, directed by Mervyn LeRoy (MGM), with Greer Garson.

§*The Lost Weekend,* 1945, directed by Billy Wilder (Paramount).

fig. 2. The Lost Weekend. Berlin, Stiftung Deutsche Kinemathek.

What I mean by thoughts and feelings "conveyed exclusively, or even primarily, by speech" is simply this: Contrary to naïve expectation, the invention of the sound track in 1928 has been unable to change the basic fact that a moving picture, even when it has learned to talk, remains a picture that moves and does not convert itself into a piece of writing that is enacted. Its substance remains a series of visual sequences held together by an uninterrupted flow of movement in space (except, of course, for such checks and pauses as have the same compositional value as a rest in music), and not a sustained study in human character and destiny transmitted by effective, let alone "beautiful," diction. I cannot remember a more misleading statement about the movies than Mr. Eric Russell Bentley's in the spring number of the *Kenyon Review,* 1945: "The potentialities of the talking screen differ from those of the silent screen in adding the dimension of dialogue—which could be poetry." I would suggest: "The potentialities of the talking screen differ from those of the silent screen in integrating visible movement with dialogue which, therefore, had better not be poetry."

All of us, if we are old enough to remember the period prior to 1928, recall the old-time pianist who, with his eyes glued on the screen, would accompany the events with music adapted to their mood and rhythm; and we also recall the weird and spectral feeling overtaking us when this pianist left his post for a few minutes and the film was allowed to run by itself, the darkness haunted by the monotonous rattle of the machinery. Even the silent film, then, was never mute. The visible spectacle always required, and received, an audible accompaniment which, from the very beginning, distinguished the film from simple pantomime and rather classed it—mutatis mutandis—with the ballet. The advent of the talkie meant not so much an "addition" as a transformation: the transformation of musical sound into articulate speech and, therefore, of quasi pantomime into an entirely new species of spectacle which differs from the ballet, and agrees with the stage play, in that its acoustic component consists of intelligible words, but differs from the stage play and agrees with the ballet in that this acoustic component is not detachable from the visual. In a film, that which we hear remains, for good or worse, inextricably fused with that which we see; the sound, articulate or not, cannot express any more than is expressed, at the same time, by visible movement; and in a good film it does not even attempt to do so. To put it briefly, the play—or, as it is very properly called, the "script"—of a moving picture is subject to what might be termed the *principle of coexpressibility.*

Empirical proof of this principle is furnished by the fact that, wherever the dialogical or monological element gains temporary prominence, there appears, with the inevitability of a natural law, the "close-up." What does the close-up achieve? In showing us, in magnification, either the face of the speaker or the face of the listeners or both in alternation, the camera transforms the human physiognomy into a huge field of action where—given the qualification of the performers—every subtle movement of the features, almost imperceptible from a natural distance, becomes an expressive event in visible space and thereby completely integrates itself with the expressive content of the spoken word; whereas, on the stage, the spoken word makes a stronger rather than a weaker impression if we are not permitted to count the hairs in Romeo's mustache.

This does not mean that the scenario is a negligible factor in the making of a moving picture. It only means that its artistic intention differs in kind from that of a stage play, and much more from that of a novel or a piece of poetry. As the success of a Gothic jamb figures depends not only upon its quality as a piece of sculpture but also, or even more so, upon its integrability with the architecture of the portal, so does the success of a movie script— not unlike that of an opera libretto—depend, not only upon its quality as a piece of literature but also, or even more so, upon its integrability with the events on the screen.

As a result—another empirical proof of the coexpressibility principle—good movie scripts are unlikely to make good reading and have seldom been published in book form; whereas, conversely, good stage plays have to be severely altered, cut, and, on the other hand, enriched by interpolations to make good movie scripts. In Shaw's *Pygmalion,** for instance, the actual process of Eliza's phonetic education and, still more important, her final triumph at the grand party, are wisely omitted; we see—or, rather, hear—some samples of her gradual linguistic improvement and finally encounter her, upon her return from the reception, victorious and splendidly arrayed but deeply hurt for want of recognition and sympathy. In the film adaptation,

---

**Pygmalion,* England 1938, directed by Anthony Asquith/Leslie Howard.*

101

precisely these two scenes are not only supplied but also strongly emphasized; we witness the fascinating activities in the laboratory with its array of spinning disks and mirrors, organ pipes, and dancing flames, and we participate in the ambassadorial party, with many moments of impending catastrophe and a little counterintrigue thrown in for suspense. Unquestionably these two scenes, entirely absent from the play, and indeed unachievable upon the stage, were the highlights of the film; whereas the Shavian dialogue, however severely cut, turned out to fall a little flat in certain moments. And wherever, as in so many other films, a poetic emotion, a musical outburst, or a literary conceit (even, I am grieved to say, some of the wisecracks of Groucho Marx) entirely lose contact with visible movement, they strike the sensitive spectator as, literally, out of place. It is certainly terrible when a soft-boiled he-man, after the suicide of his mistress, casts a twelve-foot glance upon her photograph and says something less-than-coexpressible to the effect that he will never forget her. But when he recites, instead, a piece of poetry as sublimely more-than-coexpressible as Romeo's monologue at the bier of Juliet, it is still worse. Reinhardt's *Midsummer Night's Dream* is probably the most unfortunate major film ever produced; and Olivier's *Henry V* (fig. 3) owes its comparative success, apart from the all but providential adaptability of this particular play, to so many tours de force that it will, God willing, remain an exception rather than set a pattern. It combines "judicious pruning" with the interpolation of pageantry, nonverbal comedy, and melodrama; it uses a device perhaps best designated as "oblique close-up" (Mr. Olivier's beautiful face inwardly listening to but not pronouncing the great soliloquy); and, most notably, it shifts between three levels of archaeological reality: a reconstruction of Elizabethan London, a reconstruction of the events of 1415 as laid down in Shakespeare's play, and the reconstruction of a performance of this play on Shakespeare's own stage. All this is perfectly legitimate; but, even so, the highest praise of the film will always come from those who, like the critic of the *New Yorker*, are not quite in sympathy with either the movies au naturel or Shakespeare au naturel.

As the writings of Conan Doyle potentially contain all modern mystery stories (except for the tough specimens of the Dashiell Hammett school), so do the films produced between 1900 and 1910 preestablish the subject matter and methods of the moving picture as we know it. This period produced the

fig. 3. *Henry V.* Frankfurt/Main, Deutsches Institut für Filmkunde.

incunabula of the Western and the crime film (Edwin S. Porter's amazing *The Great Train Robbery* [fig. 4] of 1903) from which developed the modern gangster, adventure, and mystery pictures (the latter, if well done, is still one of the most honest and genuine forms of film entertainment, space being doubly charged with time as the beholder asks himself not only "What is going to happen?" but also "What has happened before?"). The same period saw the emergence of the fantastically imaginative film (Méliès), which was to lead to the expressionist and surrealist experiments (*The Cabinet of Dr. Caligari, Sang d'un Poète*, etc.), on the one hand, and to the more superficial and spectacular fairy tales à la Arabian Nights, on the other. Comedy, later to triumph in Charlie Chaplin, the still insufficiently appreciated Buster Keaton, the Marx Brothers, and the pre-Hollywood creations of René Clair, reached a respectable level in Max Linder and others. In historical and melodramatic films the foundations were laid for movie iconography and movie symbolism, and in the early work of D. W. Griffith we find not only remarkable attempts at psychological analysis (*Edgar Allan Poe*) and social criticism (*A Corner in Wheat* [fig. 5]*) but also such basic technical innovations as the long shot, the flashback, and the close-up. And modest trick films and cartoons paved the way to Felix the Cat (fig. 6), Popeye the Sailor, and Felix's prodigious offspring, Mickey Mouse.

Within their self-imposed limitations the earlier Disney films, and certain sequences in the later ones,[1] represent, as it were, a chemically pure distillation of cinematic possibilities. They retain the most important folkloristic elements—sadism, pornography, the humor engendered by both, and moral justice—almost without dilution and often fuse these elements into a variation on the primitive and inexhaustible David-and-Goliath motif, the triumph of the seemingly weak over the seemingly strong; and their fantastic independence of the natural laws gives them the power to integrate space with time to such perfection that the spatial and temporal experiences of sight and hearing come to be almost interconvertible. A series of soap bubbles, successively punctured, emits a series of sounds exactly corresponding in pitch and volume to the size of the bubbles; the three uvulae of Willie the Whale—small, large, and medium—vibrate in consonance with tenor, bass, and baritone notes; and the very concept of stationary existence is com-

---

*Both 1909.

fig. 4. *The Great Train Robbery.* Berlin, Stiftung Deutsche Kinemathek.

fig. 5. *A Corner in Wheat.* Munich, Helmut Färber.

fig. 6.   *Felix, the Cat.* Frankfurt/Main, Deutsches Institut für Filmkunde.

pletely abolished. No object in creation, whether it be a house, a piano, a tree, or an alarm clock, lacks the faculties of organic, in fact anthropomorphic, movement, facial expression, and phonetic articulation. Incidentally, even in normal, "realistic" films the inanimate object, provided that it is dynamizable, can play the role of a leading character as do the ancient railroad engines in Buster Keaton's *The General* (fig. 7) and *Niagara Falls*. How the earlier Russian films exploited the possibility of heroizing all sorts of machinery lives in everybody's memory; and it is perhaps more than an accident that the two films which will go down in history as the great comical and the great serious masterpiece of the silent period bear the names and immortalize the personalities of two big ships: Keaton's *The Navigator* (1924) (fig. 8) and Eisenstein's *Battleship Potemkin* (1925) (fig. 9).

The evolution from the jerky beginnings to this grand climax offers the fascinating spectacle of a new artistic medium gradually becoming conscious of its legitimate, that is, exclusive, possibilities and limitations—a spectacle not unlike the development of the mosaic, which started out with transposing illusionistic genre pictures into a more durable material and culminated in the hieratic supernaturalism of Ravenna; or the development of line engraving, which started out as a cheap and handy substitute for book illumination and culminated in the purely "graphic" style of Dürer.

Just so the silent movies developed a definite style of their own, adapted to the specific conditions of the medium. A hitherto unknown language was forced upon a public not yet capable of reading it, and the more proficient the public became the more refinement could develop in the language. For a Saxon peasant of around 800 it was not easy to understand the meaning of a picture showing a man as he pours water over the head of another man, and even later many people found it difficult to grasp the significance of two ladies standing behind the throne of an emperor. For the public of around 1910 it was no less difficult to understand the meaning of the speechless action in a moving picture, and the producers employed means of clarification similar to those we find in medieval art. One of these were printed titles or letters, striking equivalents of the medieval *tituli* and scrolls (at a still earlier date there even used to be explainers who would say, viva voce, "Now he thinks his wife is dead but she isn't" or "I don't wish to offend the ladies in the audience but I doubt that any of them would have done that much for her child"). Another, less obtrusive method of explanation was the

fig. 7. *The General.* Frankfurt/Main, Deutsches Institut für Filmkunde.

fig. 8. *The Navigator.* Berlin, Stiftung Deutsche Kinemathek.

fig. 9.   Battleship Potemkin. Berlin, Stiftung Deutsche Kinemathek.

introduction of a fixed iconography which from the outset informed the spectator about the basic facts and characters, much as the two ladies behind the emperor, when carrying a sword and a cross, respectively, were uniquely determined as Fortitude and Faith. There arose, identifiable by standardized appearance, behavior, and attributes, the well-remembered types of the Vamp and the Straight Girl (perhaps the most convincing modern equivalents of the medieval personifications of the Vices and Virtues), the Family Man, and the Villain, the latter marked by a black mustache and walking stick. Nocturnal scenes were printed on blue or green film. A checkered tablecloth meant, once for all, a "poor but honest" milieu; a happy marriage, soon to be endangered by the shadows from the past, was symbolized by the young wife's pouring the breakfast coffee for her husband; the first kiss was invariably announced by the lady's gently playing with her partner's necktie and was invariably accompanied by her kicking out with her left foot. The conduct of the characters was predetermined accordingly. The poor but honest laborer who, after leaving his little house with the checkered tablecloth, came upon an abandoned baby could not but take it to his home and bring it up as best he could; the Family Man could not but yield, however temporarily, to the temptations of the Vamp. As a result these early melodramas had a highly gratifying and soothing quality in that events took shape, without the complications of individual psychology, according to a pure Aristotelian logic so badly missed in real life.

Devices like these became gradually less necessary as the public grew accustomed to interpreting the action by itself and were virtually abolished by the invention of the talking film. But even now there survive—quite legitimately, I think—the remnants of a "fixed attitude and attribute" principle and, more basic, a primitive or folkloristic concept of plot construction. Even today we take it for granted that the diphtheria of a baby tends to occur when the parents are out and, having occurred, solves all their matrimonial problems. Even today we demand of a decent mystery film that the butler, though he may be anything from an agent of the British Secret Service to the real father of the daughter of the house, must not turn out to be the murderer. Even today we love to see Pasteur, Zola, or Ehrlich win out against stupidity and wickedness, with their respective wives trusting and trusting all the time. Even today we much prefer a happy finale to a gloomy one and insist, at the very least, on the observance of the Aristotelian rule that the story have a beginning, a middle, and an ending—a rule the abrogation of which has done so much to estrange the general public from the more elevated spheres of modern writing. Primitive symbolism, too, survives in such amusing details as the last sequence of *Casablanca* where the delightfully crooked and right-minded *préfet de police* casts an empty bottle of Vichy water into the wastepaper basket; and in such telling symbols of the supernatural as Sir Cedric Hardwicke's Death in a the guise of a "gentleman in a dustcoat trying" (*On Borrowed Time*)* or Claude Rains's Hermes Psychopompos in the striped trousers of an airline manager (*Here Comes Mr. Jordan* [fig. 10]).†

The most conspicuous advances were made in directing, lighting, camera work, cutting, and acting proper. But while in most of these fields the evolution proceeded continuously—though, of course, not without detours, breakdowns, and archaic relapses—the development of acting suffered a sudden interruption by the invention of the talking film; so that the style of acting in the silents can already be evaluated in retrospect, as a lost art not unlike the painting technique of Jan van Eyck or, to take up our previous simile, the burin technique of Dürer. It was soon realized that acting in a silent film neither meant a pantomimic exaggeration of stage acting (as was generally and erroneously assumed by professional stage actors who more and more frequently condescended to perform in the movies), nor could dispense with stylization altogether; a man photographed while walking down a gangway in ordinary, everyday-life fashion looked like anything but a man walking down a gangway when the result appeared on the screen. If the picture was to look both natural and meaningful the acting had to be done in a manner equally different from the style of the stage and the reality of ordinary life; speech had to be made dispensable by establishing an organic relation between the acting and the technical procedure of cinephotography—much as in Dürer's prints color had been made dispensable by establishing an organic relation between the design and the technical procedure of line engraving.

On Borrowed Time, 1939, directed by Harold S. Bucquet (MGM). The line "I am a gentleman in a dustcoat trying" opens a very good poem by John Crowe Ransom (1888–1974), which also expresses a conception of death. —Note added by Panofsky in a German translation of the essay that appeared in *Filmkritik* 11, 1967, 343–55, trans. by Ed.

†*Here Comes Mr. Jordan*, 1941, directed by Alexander Hall (Columbia).

fig. 10. Here Comes Mr. Jordan. Berlin, Stiftung Deutsche Kinemathek.

This was precisely what the great actors of the silent period accomplished, and it is a significant fact that the best of them did not come from the stage, whose crystallized tradition prevented Duse's only film, *Cenere*, from being more than a priceless record of Duse. The came instead from the circus or the variety, as was the case of Chaplin, Keaton, and Will Rogers; from nothing in particular, as was the case of Theda Bara, of her greater European parallel, the Danish actress Asta Nielsen, and of Garbo; or from everything under the sun, as was the case of Douglas Fairbanks. The style of these "old masters" was indeed comparable to the style of line engraving in that it was, and had to be, exaggerated in comparison with stage acting (just as the sharply incised and vigorously curved *tailles* of the burin are exaggerated in comparison with pencil strokes or brushwork), but richer, subtler, and infinitely more precise. The advent of the talkies, reducing if not abolishing this difference between screen acting and stage acting, thus confronted the actors and actresses of the silent screen with a serious problem. Buster Keaton yielded to temptation and fell. Chaplin first tried to stand his ground and to remain an exquisite archaist but finally gave in, with only moderate success (*The Great Dictator*). Only the glorious Harpo has thus far successfully refused to utter a single articulate sound; and only Greta Garbo succeeded, in a measure, in transforming her style in principle. But even in her case one cannot help feeling that her first talking picture, *Anna Christie*, where she could ensconce herself, most of the time, in mute or monosyllabic sullenness, was better than her later performances; and in the second, talking version of *Anna Karenina* (fig. 11), the weakest moment is certainly when she delivers a big Ibsenian speech to her husband, and the strongest when she silently moves along the platform of the railroad station while her despair takes shape in the consonance of her movement (and expression) with the movement of the nocturnal space around her, filled with the real noises of the trains and the imaginary sound of the "little men with the iron hammers" that drives her, relentlessly and almost without her realizing it, under the wheels.

Small wonder that there is sometimes felt a kind of nostalgia for the silent period and that devices have been worked out to combine the virtues of sound and speech with those of silent acting, such as the oblique close-up already mentioned in connection with *Henry V;* the dance behind glass doors in *Sous les Toits de Paris;* or, in the *Histoire d'un Tricheur,* Sacha Guitry's recital of the events of his youth while the events themselves are "silently" enacted on the screen. However, this nostalgic feeling is no argument against the talkies as such. Their evolution has shown that, in art, every gain entails a certain loss on the other side of the ledger; but that the gain remains a gain, provided that the basic nature of the medium is realized and respected. One can imagine that, when the cavemen of Altamira began to paint their buffaloes in natural colors instead of merely incising the contours, the more conservative cavemen foretold the end of paleolithic art. But paleolithic art went on, and so will the movies. New technical inventions always tend to dwarf the values already attained, especially in a medium that owes its very existence to technical experimentation. The earliest talkies were infinitely inferior to the then mature silents, and most of the present technicolor films are still inferior to the now mature talkies in black and white. But even if Aldous Huxley's nightmare should come true and the experiences of taste, smell, and touch should be added to those of sight and hearing, even then we may say with the Apostle, as we have said when first confronted with the soundtrack and the technicolor film, "We are troubled on every side, yet not distressed; we are perplexed, but not in despair."

From the law of time-charged space and space-bound time, there follows the fact that the screenplay, in contrast to the theater play, *has no aesthetic existence independent of its performance, and that its characters have no aesthetic existence outside the actors.*

The playwright writes in the fond hope that his work will be an imperishable jewel in the treasure house of civilization and will be presented in hundreds of performances that are but transient variations on a "work" that is constant. The scriptwriter, on the other hand, writes for one producer, one director, and one cast. Their work achieves the same degree of permanence as does his; and should the same or a similar scenario ever be filmed by a different director and a different cast there will result an altogether different "play."

Othello or Nora are definite, substantial figures created by the playwright. They can be played well or badly, and they can be "interpreted" in one way or another; but they most definitely exist, no matter who plays them or even whether they are played at all. The character in a film, however, lives and dies with the actor. It is not the entity "Othello" interpreted by Robeson or the entity "Nora" interpreted by Duse; it is the entity "Greta Garbo" incarnate in a figure called Anne Christie or the entity "Robert Montgomery"

fig. 11. *Anna Karenina.* Berlin, Stiftung Deutsche Kinemathek.

incarnate in a murderer who, for all we know or care to know, may forever remain anonymous but will never cease to haunt our memories. Even when the names of the characters happen to be Henry VIII or Anna Karenina, the king who ruled England from 1509 to 1547 and the woman created by Tolstoy, they do not exist outside the being of Garbo and Laughton. They are but empty and incorporeal outlines like the shadows in Homer's Hades, assuming the character of reality only when filled with the lifeblood of an actor. Conversely, if a movie role is badly played there remains literally nothing of it, no matter how interesting the character's psychology or how elaborate the words.

What applies to the actor applies, mutatis mutandis, to most of the other artists, or artisans, who contribute to the making of a film: the director, the sound man, the enormously important cameraman, even the makeup man. A stage production is rehearsed until everything is ready, and then it is repeatedly performed in three consecutive hours. At each performance everybody has to be on hand and does his work; and afterward he goes home and to bed. The work of the stage actor may thus be likened to that of a musician, and that of the stage director to that of a conductor. Like these, they have a certain repertoire which they have studied and present in a number of complete but transitory performances, be it *Hamlet* today and *Ghosts* tomorrow, or *Life with Father per saecula saeculorum.** The activities of the film actor and the film director, however, are comparable, respectively, to those of the plastic artist and the architect, rather than to those of the musician and the conductor. Stage work is continuous but transitory; film work is discontinuous but permanent. Individual sequences are done piecemeal and out of order according to the most efficient use of sets and personnel. Each bit is done over and over again until it stands; and when the whole has been cut and composed everyone is through with it forever. Needless to say that this very procedure cannot but emphasize the curious consubstantiality that exists between the person of the movie actor and his role. Coming into existence piece by piece, regardless of the natural sequence of events, the "character" can grow into a unified whole only if the actor manages to be, not merely to

---

**Life with Father was (or is) the title of a comedy by Clarence Day, published by his widow, that had an unprecedented success in America, and hence was performed "through all eternity." —Note added by Panofsky in a German translation of the essay that appeared in *Filmkritik* 11, 1967, 343–55, trans. by Ed.

play, Henry VIII or Anna Karenina throughout the entire wearisome period of shooting. I have it on the best of authorities that Laughton was really difficult to live with in the particular six or eight weeks during which he was doing—or rather being—Captain Bligh.

It might be said that a film, called into being by a cooperative effort in which all contributions have the same degree of permanence, is the nearest modern equivalent of a medieval cathedral; the role of the producer corresponding, more or less, to that of the bishop or archbishop; that of the director to that of the architect in chief; that of the scenario writers to that of the scholastic advisers establishing the iconographical program; and that of the actors, cameramen, cutters, sound men, makeup men, and the divers technicians to that of those whose work provided the physical entity of the finished product, from the sculptors, glass painters, bronze casters, carpenters, and skilled masons down to the quarry men and woodsmen. And if you speak to any one of these collaborators he will tell you, with perfect bona fides, that his is really the most important job—which is quite true to the extent that it is indispensable.

This comparison may seem sacrilegious, not only because there are, proportionally, fewer good films than there are good cathedrals, but also because the movies are commercial. However, if commercial art be defined as all art not primarily produced in order to gratify the creative urge of its maker but primarily intended to meet the requirements of a patron or a buying public, it must be said that noncommercial art is the exception rather than the rule, and a fairly recent and not always felicitous exception at that. While it is true that commercial art is always in danger of ending up as a prostitute, it is equally true that noncommercial art is always in danger of ending up as an old maid. Noncommercial art has given us Seurat's "Grande Jatte" and Shakespeare's sonnets, but also much that is esoteric to the point of incommunicability. Conversely, commercial art has given us much that is vulgar or snobbish (two aspects of the same thing) to the point of loathsomeness, but also Dürer's prints and Shakespeare's plays. For, we must not forget that Dürer's prints were partly made on commission and partly intended to be sold in the open market; and that Shakespeare's plays—in contrast to the earlier masques and intermezzi which were produced at court by aristocratic amateurs and could afford to be so incomprehensible that even those who described them in printed monographs occasionally failed to grasp their intended significance—were meant to appeal, and did appeal, not only to the select few but also to everyone who was prepared to pay a shilling for admission.

It is this requirement of communicability that makes commercial art more vital than noncommercial, and therefore potentially much more effective for better or for worse. The commercial producer can both educate and pervert the general public, and can allow the general public—or rather his idea of the general public—both to educate and to pervert himself. As is demonstrated by a number of excellent films that proved to be great box office successes, the public does not refuse to accept good products if it gets them. That it does not get them very often is caused not so much by commercialism as such as by too little discernment and, paradoxical though it may seem, too much timidity in its application. Hollywood believes that it must produce "what the public wants" while the public would take whatever Hollywood produces. If Hollywood were to decide for itself what it wants it would get away with it—even if it should decide to "depart from evil and do good." For, to revert to whence we started, in modern life the movies are what most other forms of art have ceased to be, not an adornment but a necessity.

That this should be so is understandable, not only from a sociological but also from an art-historical point of view. The processes of all the earlier representational arts conform, in a higher or lesser degree, to an idealistic conception of the world. These arts operate from top to bottom, so to speak, and not from bottom to top; they start with an idea to be projected into shapeless matter and not with the objects that constitute the physical world. The painter works on a blank wall or canvas which he organizes into a likeness of things and persons according to his idea (however much this idea may have been nourished by reality); he does not work with the things and persons themselves even if he works "from the model." The same is true of the sculptor with his shapeless mass of clay or his untooled block of stone or wood; of the writer with his sheet of paper or his dictaphone; and even of the stage designer with his empty and sorely limited section of space. It is the movies, and only the movies, that do justice to that materialistic interpretation of the universe which, whether we like it or not, pervades contemporary civilization. Excepting the very special case of the animated cartoon, the movies organize material things and persons, not a neutral medium, into a composition that receive its style, and may even become fantastic or pretervoluntarily

fig. 12.   *The Cabinet of Dr. Caligari.* Frankfurt/Main, Deutsches Institut für Filmkunde.

symbolic,[2] not so much by an interpretation in the artist's mind as by the actual manipulation of physical objects and recording machinery. The medium of the movies is physical reality as such: the physical reality of eighteenth-century Versailles—no matter whether it be the original or a Hollywood facsimile indistinguishable therefrom for all aesthetic intents and purposes—or of a suburban home in Westchester; the physical reality of the Rue de Lappe in Paris or of the Gobi Desert, of Paul Ehrlich's apartment in Frankfurt or of the streets of New York in the rain; the physical reality of engines and animals, of Edward G. Robinson and Jimmy Cagney. All these objects and persons must be organized into a work of art. They can be arranged in all sorts of ways ("arrangement" comprising, of course, such things as make-up, lighting, and camera work); but there is no running away from them. From this point of view it becomes evident that an attempt at subjecting the world to artistic prestylization, as in the expressionist settings of *The Cabinet of Dr. Caligari* (1919) (fig. 12), could be no more than an exciting experiment that could exert but little influence upon the general course of events. To prestylize reality prior to tackling it amounts to dodging the problem. The problem is to manipulate and shoot unstylized reality in such a way that the result has style. This is a proposition no less legitimate and no less difficult than any proposition in the older arts.

fig. 13. Ponchielli's "Dance of the Hours" in *Fantasia*. Berlin, Stiftung Deutsche Kinemathek. *See note 1.*

fig. 14. Beethoven's "Pastorale" in *Fantasia*. Berlin, Stiftung Deutsche Kinemathek. *See note 1.*

fig. 15. *A Night in Casablanca.* Berlin, Stiftung Deutsche Kinemathek. *See note 2.*

III

The Ideological Antecedents of the Rolls-Royce Radiator

Erwin Panofsky

I.

Without going so far as Thomas Gray, who said of the English people that "the only proof of their original talent in matters of pleasure is their skill in gardening and laying out of grounds," we must admit that one of the greatest British contributions to European art is that "Garden Revolution" which, from the second decade of the eighteenth century, replaced the formal Italo-French garden of the preceding era with what is called an "English Garden" in all languages: "Englischer Garten" in German, "Jardin Anglais" in French and "Giardino Inglese" in Italian.[1]

The "formal" style of gardening, reaching its climax in Le Nôtre's Versailles, had proudly imposed upon the infinity and irregularity of nature the finiteness and order of a little universe conceived by man—a universe cut out of (and off from) the great outdoors and rationally organized into a geometrical pattern of avenues suitable for the stately progress of carriages and the caperings of horsemen rather than for solitary walks, parterres designed after the fashion of oriental carpets, trees and hedges carefully clipped into stereometrical shapes, "mazes" which pose neat problems in topology, and bodies of water disciplined to the regular contours of basins and canals (fig. 1).

Shaftesbury, in *The Moralist* (1709), seems to have been the first to stress the basic contrast between such "tailored" gardens and untouched nature "where neither Art nor the Conceit or Caprice of Man has spoiled" the "genuine order" of God's creation. "Even the rude Rocks," he feels, "the mossy Cavern, the irregular unwrought Grottoes, and broken Falls of Waters, with all the horrid Graces of the Wilderness itself, as representing Nature more, will be more engaging, and appeal with a Magnificance beyond the formal Mockery of princely Gardens." It took only one further step to postulate that the gardens themselves conform to the "genuine order of nature" instead of contradicting it. Where Le Nôtre had said that good gardens must not look like woods, Joseph Addison in the *Spectator* of 1712 painted the image of an ideal garden which conforms to the laws of "nature unadorned" (as Pope was to express it seven years later). He prefers wild flowers to plants artificially bred and finds it delightful "not to know whether the next tree will be an apple, an oak, an elm, or a pear." He "would rather look upon a tree in all its abundance and diffusion of boughs and branches, than when it is cut and trimmed into a mathematical figure"; and he "cannot but fancy that an orchard in flower looks infinitely more delightful than all the little labyrinths of the most finished parterre."

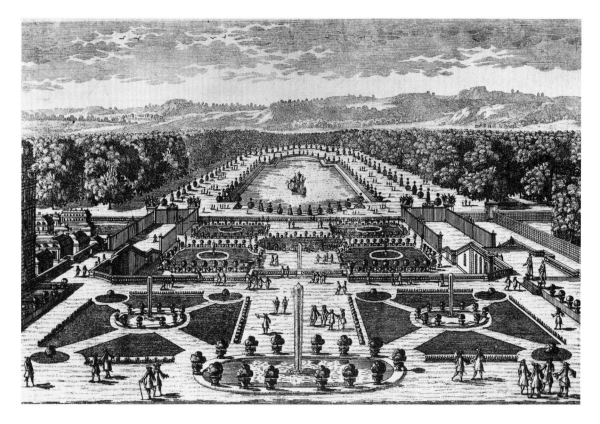

fig. 1.   Garden at Versailles, engraving at Aveline.

To conceive of a garden as a piece of "nature unadorned" is of course a contradiction in terms; for, as Sir Joshua Reynolds was judiciously to remark in his *Discourses on Art*, "if the true taste consists, as many hold, in banishing every appearance of Art or any traces of the footsteps of man, it would then be no longer a garden."[2] He therefore prefers the definition of a garden as "Nature to advantage dress'd"; and it was this concept (well expressed by Pope when he admonishes the gardener "to treat the Goddess [Nature] like a modest Fair, / Nor overdress nor leave her wholly bare")[3] which was to govern the practice of the great English gardeners of the eighteenth century from Bridgeman, the original designer of Stowe (credited with the significant invention of the so-called Ha-ha, the sunken wall or fence which encloses and protects the garden without visibly separating it from the surrounding countryside) through William Kent, "the true father of modern gardening" (who finished Stowe and designed Kew and Kensington Gardens, and of whom Horace Walpole in his *Essay on Modern Gardens* was to say that, "while Mahomet imagined one Elysium, Kent created many") to Lancelot ("Capability") Brown, who dominated the scene up to his death in 1783 (figs. 2, 3).

Yet, even when "to advantage dress'd," nature remains nature. The new English garden with its rolling lawns, its seemingly casual though artfully arranged clumps of trees, its ponds and brooks, and its serpentine footpaths (Kent made it axiomatic that "nature abhors a straight line") retains and accentuates precisely those "natural" values which the formal garden intended to suppress: the qualities of picturesque variety, surprise, and apparent infinitude ("He gains all points," says Pope, "who pleasingly confounds, / Surprises, varies and conceals the bounds");[4] and, consequently, the power of appealing to the emotions instead of gratifying the sense of objective and rational order. In his *Elements of Criticism* (1762) Henry Home (Lord Kames) maintains the superiority of gardening over architecture because the gardener, presenting us with a succession of different prospects, is able to evoke an infinite variety of emotions where the architect is limited to inspiring the feelings of beauty and grandeur;[5] and how conducive these emotional potentialities of the new English garden were to downright sentimentality was demonstrated—exactly forty years before the appearance of Lord Kames's book—in Alexander Pope's answer to John Gay's congratulations on the completion of Pope's famous garden at Twickenham:

Ah, friend! 'tis true—this truth you lovers know—
In vain my structures rise, my gardens grow . . .

fig. 2. Park at Stowe, Buckinghamshire. Buckingham, Buckinghamshire, Stow School.

fig. 3.   Park at Stowe, bird's-eye view. Buckingham, Buckinghamshire, Stow School.

What are the gray Parterre, the chequer'd Shade,
The morning Bower, the ev'ning Colonnade
But soft recesses of uneasy minds
To sigh unheard into the passing winds?
So the struck deer in some sequester'd part
Lies down to die, the arrow in his heart.

In words like these there shines, indeed, to quote Pope's own words, "a light which in yourself you must perceive; / Jones and Le Nôtre have it not to give."[6]

II.

Small wonder that the "modern" garden, symbolic of the "all-bearing earth" in its entirety, tended from the outset to be strewn with incidental architectural features (*tempietti*, "follies," towers, bridges, even artificial ruins) the style of which reflects all kinds of "taste"—from the classical or would-be classical to the "Egyptian," the "Chinese" (fig. 4), the "Gothick" or the "rustic"; whereby we may remember that the Gothic style was looked upon as something derived from "untouched nature," its pointed arches, noncolumnar supports, and crisp or curly tracery being believed to derive from unsquared trees. And yet the serious secular architecture of the period, both in town and country, was dominated by a movement diametrically opposed to the subjective and emotional: Palladian classicism. This "Palladianism,"[7] temporarily sidetracked by the more Baroque inclinations of Christopher Wren (1632–1723) and John Vanbrugh (1664–1726), had been initiated by the same Inigo Jones (1573–1652) whom Pope aligns with Le Nôtre, and it was not only revived but dogmatized at the same time and in the same illustrious circles which produced the "Garden Revolution."

The most important of these circles was that of Henry Boyle, Third Earl of Burlington (1694–1753). Designer and/or *spiritus rector* of numerous severely classicizing structures (his town house was built by himself in cooperation with his mentor, Colin Campbell, the author of the *Vitruvius Britannicus*), he was sufficiently appreciative of Inigo Jones to acquire and to re-erect the battered gateway of the latter's Beaufort House in Chelsea.[8] Literally in love with Palladio, he undertook a special trip to Vicenza and its environs to familiarize himself with the old master's works; he designed the house of a friend, General Wade, after a Palladio drawing in his own possession; and about the same time (1723–25) he patterned his own country

fig. 4. Die Pagoda in the Royal Gardens at Kew. London, British Library.

house, Chiswick (fig. 5), after the model of Palladio's Villa Rotonda,[9] built about 175 years before (fig. 6) and in turn harking back to the Pantheon.

Yet this austere Palladian most intimately collaborated with William Kent. While as an architect Kent inclined to share, occasionally even to surpass, the classicistic leanings of his high-born friend,[10] he indulged in distinctly "Baroque" inventions as an interior decorator; and he was, we recall, the most advanced among the contemporary garden designers. Thus Burlington's Chiswick, like most important country seats of the time, combines an uncompromisingly "classical" style of architecture with an essentially modern treatment of the surrounding grounds. In fact, the garden at Chiswick was laid out, in 1717, in strictly "formal" manner and "anglicized," as far as possible, only while the Palladian villa was being built from ca. 1725.

III.

With some modifications but essentially unabated, this antinomy persisted in the following phase of English architecture which was largely dominated by Robert Adam (1728–92) and his brothers. This "Adam style"—which, at the hands of a Jacques-Ange Gabriel, was to develop into the "style Louis XVI" on the Continent[11]—is a successful attempt to reconcile the orthodox Palladianism of the Burlingtons and Campbells with the style of Vanbrugh, and the result has happily been termed "picturesque classicism": Palladianism was adapted to the requirements of a still stately but more intimate habitability; and its austerity was enlivened by the opulent grace of Roman decoration recently popularized by the discovery of Herculaneum.

At the same time, however, at which Robert Adam erected the very "classical" North Pavilion of Hopetoun House (fig. 7, 1752)[12] or the Great Hall at Castle Ashby (1759, when his style had reached its characteristic maturity),[13] he designed "Gothick" bridges, towers, "follies," and churches (fig. 8).[14] He was fond of inventing artificial ruins,[15] and the impression of the Rhenish churches, representing that mixture of Romanesque and Gothic elements which has come to be known, not very accurately, as "Rheinischer Uebergangsstil," inspired him, in December 1757, with a fantasy as picturesque and florid as anything devised in the nineteenth century (fig. 9).[16]

The same decade (1760–70) which saw the first systematic exploration of Greek and "Etruscan" vase painting also saw the publication of Ossian and *The Castle of Otranto*. The term "sublime"—with its implications of transcendency in relation to the accepted standards of formal beauty and rational

fig. 5. Chiswick House, Chiswick, Middlesex. Bildarchiv Foto Marburg.

fig. 6. La Rotonda, Vicenza. Bildarchiv Foto Marburg.

fig. 7. John and Robert Adam, Hopetoun House. London, Courtauld Institute of Art.

fig. 8.   Robert Adam, drawing for a "Folly." Private collection.

fig. 9.   Robert Adam, fantastic medieval building. London, Sir John Sloane's Museum.

comprehensibility—began to be transferred from literature and natural scenery to art—with the result that the cool classicism of a Gavin Hamilton was opposed by a host of painters specializing in highly inflammatory, often intentionally horrid subjects;[17] and the epithet "sublime" came to be applied to Michelangelo whom England can claim to have rescued from the disapprobation of the continental academies.[18]

In short, the English eighteenth century stands, at one and the same time, both far to the right and far to the left of contemporary developments on the Continent: a severely formal rationalism, tending to look for support to classical antiquity, contrasts but coexists with a highly subjective emotionalism, drawing inspiration from fancy, nature, and the medieval past, which, for want of a better expression, may be described as "Romantic." And this antinomy of opposite principles—analogous to the fact that social and institutional life in England is more strictly controlled by tradition and convention, yet gives more scope to individual "eccentricity" than anywhere else—can be observed throughout the history of English art and letters.

IV.

Among the most impressive and engaging English inventions, for example, are the drolleries disporting themselves on the margins of illuminated manuscripts from ca. 1250 (fig. 10).[19] Based on the fables or the exempla used by preachers but as often derived from actual experience or sheer imagination, these drolleries foreshadow Hogarth and Rawlinson as well as Jerome Bosch; they run the whole gamut from sharply observed reality to the grotesque, the scurrilous, and the phantasmagoric. And when they crossed the Channel they were most eagerly accepted and developed in the regions adjacent to it, namely, in northeastern France and in the Netherlands. But while the continental artists—particularly those who, like the great Jean Pucelle, adapted the new vogue to the refined taste of the Royal Domain—attempted, as far as the mode of presentation was concerned, to reconcile the style of the marginal drolleries with that of the principal pictures, a sharp dichotomy can be observed in England. In the same schools in which we find the drolleries at their liveliest, at times even in the same manuscript, the principal pictures are dominated by a solemn formality approaching the hieratic. The earliest datable manuscript exhibiting full-fledged drolleries, the Rutland Psalter at Belvoir Castle executed for Edmund de Laci or de Lacey, Earl of Lincoln

fig. 10. The Rutland Psalter. London, British Library.

(d. 1257 or 1258), contains a *Christ in Majesty* more strictly formalized and unapproachable than anything produced on the Continent at the same time (fig. 11).[20]

The following century—the century that witnessed the victories of Crécy and Poitiers and the reemergence of English as the language of the nobles, the educated and the law courts[21]—produced three important and nearly contemporary innovations in the domain of Gothic architecture which may be said to epitomize the two contrastive principles here under discussion, the first representing a triumph of the irrational; the second a triumph of the rational; the third a triumph of both.

Throughout the thirteenth century English architecture, like that on the Continent, was essentially dominated by straight lines and "simple" curves, that is to say, circular arcs. It was in England that these "simple" curves began to be replaced by "compound" curves, each of them resulting from the merger of at least one convex with at least one concave element. The result was the "decorated," "flowing" or—to call it by its most usual though not very accurate name—"curvilinear" style which flourished in England from ca. 1320 to the end of the century and played an important part in the formation of the "Flamboyant" phase of the Gothic style on the Continent.[22] The examples of this "curvilinear" style, such as the "Bishop's Eye" of Lincoln Cathedral (executed shortly after 1319),[23] the east window of Hawton (second quarter of the fourteenth century) or the somewhat later east window of Carlisle, the curves of which are said to require the plotting of no less than 263 circles,[24] give the impression of an ordered chaos comparable to those "close-knit and involved intricacies" of early insular ornamentation[25] a dim recollection of which may indeed have played a part in the emergence of this type of tracery (fig. 12).

But only a few years after the formation of the "curvilinear" style there arose a countermovement so resolutely rational and sober-minded that it was never accepted on the other side of the Channel: the "perpendicular style." Announcing itself in St. Stephen's Chapel in Westminster Palace, it appears fully developed in the choir, south transept, and cloisters of Gloucester Cathedral, all started in the fourth decade of the fourteenth century.[26] In an attempt to obtain a maximum of window space with a minimum of effort and expense (so that "so much more window could be had for the same money"), but also, I believe, in deference to the second, "rightist" trend occasionally suppressed but never absent on English soil, the tracery was simpli-

fig. 11. The Rutland Psalter, *Majestus Domini*. London, British Library.

fig. 12.   Church at Hawton, Nottinghamshire, east window. London, Courtauld Institute of Art.

fied into a uniform grill composed, in principle, of rectangular fields—the only remaining curves being the trefoil arches which convert each of the rectangles into a little "niche" suitable for the reception of a single figure (fig. 13). What had been an intricate pattern of tracery, its irregular interstices precariously filled with glass, became an expanse of glass neatly divided by a system of coordinates. But the two systems coexisted for many decades until the perpendicular style won out to hold sway up to the belated advent of the Italian Renaissance.

Simultaneously with the perpendicular style there came into being the third of the innovations alluded to above (it, too, rejected on the Continent): the fan vault which, to the non-English eye, gives the impression of a *monde renversé* (fig. 14).[27] It differs from the normal Gothic rib vault in that it does not consist of spherical triangles of different sizes (the transverse arches being longer than the longitudinal ones, and the diagonal arches being longer than both) but of congruent, inverted conoids which can be constructed by rotating one curve (viz., half of a "four-centered arch") around a vertical axis and may be decorated with equidistant radial ribs of equal length. Where the normal Gothic rib vault culminates in a keystone, the apex of a fan vault forms a plateaulike surface delimited by the bases of the conoids; and, to make this inversion of the normal situation doubly conspicuous, the English builders liked to drop from these "plateaus" huge pendants which tend to produce an effect not unlike that of stalactites (fig. 15).

Yet, when stripped to its structural essentials, this apparently fantastic, even topsy-turvy vaulting system reveals itself to be no less practical and economical than is the perpendicular organization of the walls and windows with which we find it normally combined and whose rigid schematism creates a strong visual contrast to its fanciful exuberance. Since all the radii of all the conoids have the same length and the same curvature, the size and shape of the *voussoirs* could be standardized. The surfaces between the conoids could be constructed from large, thin panels. And the comparative flatness and lightness of the whole system, combined with the more important fact that conoids, in contrast to rib vaults, exert a downward rather than lateral thrust, greatly reduced the deformative forces operating in a normal Gothic vault. As a result (even in such extreme cases as the Chapel of Henry VII), the use of fan vaults permits a maximum of fenestration and requires a minimum of buttressing.

fig. 13. Cathedral of Gloucester, choir. London, Courtauld Institute of Art.

fig. 14. Cathedral of Gloucester, cloister, south arcade. London, Courtauld Institute of Art.

fig. 15. Westminster Abbey, Chapel of Henry VII. London, Courtauld Institute of Art.

This uncanny sense of practicality (even where it conceals itself behind an almost paradoxical appearance) is a third and very important aspect of the English character—the character of a nation both "romantic" and conservative yet rightly renowned for its positivistic outlook and blessed with a special aptitude for craftsmanship and technical invention. We may remember that, while the Burlingtons and Campbells developed their orthodox Palladianism, while the Adams evolved their "picturesque" version of classicism, and while the Bridgemans, Kents, and Browns laid out their modern, sentimental gardens, the Newcomens, Cowleys, and Watts devised and perfected the steam engine and the Lewis Pauls, Hargreaves, Cromptons, and Arkwrights developed the spinning machine.

V.

Where the times were propitious, the rationalistic or conservative tendency in English art sought, we recall, support and nourishment in classical antiquity. This applies not only to the Palladian revival—or, rather, revivals—but also to the very beginnings of insular art where Mediterranean influences can be observed in the Northumbrian crosses and such manuscripts as the Codex Amiatinus, the Lindisfarne Gospels, or the Gospels of Maaseyck—the earliest Northern attempts at reviving a humanistic concept of man in art. But even at this early stage a tension can be felt between the diluted classicality of the Early Christian forms ultimately derived from Hellenistic prototypes and a barbaric, antihumanistic tendency, particularly potent in the ornamental features, which seems to be rooted in an aboriginal Celtic, particularly Irish tradition.[28]

The name of Ireland raises the question as to how we can explain this curious and persistent antinomy which, as I phrased it, places English art both far to the right and far to the left of Continental developments. This is one of those questions which the historian cannot hope to answer—and is perhaps not even entitled to pose—but cannot help musing about. First of all, England, an island unusually vulnerable to occupation up to the Norman Conquest but practically impervious to attack ever after, was always conscious of its "distance" from the rest of Europe. Second (and consequently), the ethnic structure of the English population was determined by the successive predominance of pre-Celtic "Iberians," Celts, Anglo-Saxons, Norsemen, and Normans; from this resulted (apart from the fact that the English language became, as it did, a unique compound of the Germanic and the Romance) a constant interaction of what has been called "wild Celtic fancy" and the "deep feeling and good sense of the Nordic races." [29] Third, in contrast to the major portions of Germany, England had been conquered by the Romans; but in contrast to Spain and France, this conquest had not resulted in a real Romanization. "The greatest fact in the early history of the island," says Trevelyan, "is a negative fact—that the Romans did not succeed in permanently Latinizing Britain as they Latinized France." [30] Fourth, England was Christianized not, as might be expected, from France but from two different quarters at once: the northern part of the country from Ireland (converted by St. Patrick as early as the second third of the fifth century), whence St. Columba, establishing himself on the Island of Iona in 563, carried Christianity to Western Scotland and Northumbria; the southern part directly from Rome whence St. Augustine and Theodore of Tarsus (the former Archbishop of Canterbury from 597, the latter from 669) arrived in Kent, once the landing place of the Roman armies. Both St. Augustine and Theodore of Tarsus brought with them not only the Christian faith, theological knowledge, and church music, but also a treasury of purely classical learning (in Theodore's case even Greek learning); and the School of Canterbury—matched in the North by such centers as Jarrow-Wearmouth and York—not only flourished but proliferated at a time when the pre-Carolingian Continent was barbarized to such an extent that Charlemagne had to call on Alcuin, a product of York, to help him with his *renovatio* of Roman art and letters.

In England, then, we have, on the one hand, a strong admixture of the Celtic element—tending towards hyperbole, involved and "nonobjective" movement and unbridled imagination—in the very centers of ecclesiastical and secular culture; and, on the other, the unparalleled continuity of a classical tradition which, upon an island far removed from the Mediterranean and never Latinized in its entirety, tended to assume the character of an "invisible lodge."

All this does not explain but may make us understand, to a degree, the characteristic antinomies of English art and civilization, especially the peculiar British attitude towards classical antiquity. In England the classical tradition was—and in a measure still is—looked upon as a part of the national heritage no less important than the Bible—yet as a realm accessible only to a privileged élite and far removed from palpable reality in space and time. Remnants of Roman buildings, recklessly mistreated by the invading Anglo-Saxons, existed but never became an integral part of the living scenery as was the case in Italy, in France and even in southwest Germany; and we can easily conceive that the English reaction to classical antiquity was either antiquarian or "romantic" or both.

It is no accident that, after the initial impact of Mediterranean art in the first millennium, the direct influence of classical models did not amount to much before the rise of scholarly archaeology;[31] while, on the other hand, in one of the earliest monuments of Anglo-Saxon literature—that amazing poem, *The Ruin*—Roman remains (presumably those of Bath) are interpreted as a symbol of the destructive forces of destiny, reducing to rubble the proudest efforts of man while yet appealing to the aesthetic perception.[32] In the twelfth and early thirteenth centuries, finally, we find, as far as classical art is concerned, an effort not at direct assimilation, as in the French and Italian "proto-Renaissance,"[33] but a most interesting mixture of connoisseurlike appreciation, collector's enthusiasm and antiquarian pedantry—all very anachronistic from a Continental point of view.

Osbert de Clare, visiting Rome as an envoy of King Stephen (d. 1154), raves about the marble images on the Arch of Titus because they are "aging throughout the centuries without any trace of oldness" ("nulla temporis vetustate per saecula senescentes")[34] and wishes that a similar monument might be erected to St. Edmund. Bishop Henry of Blois, sojourning in Rome in 1151, bought up (*coemit*) a great number of classical statues "contrived by the heathens in subtle and laborious rather than devout error" and had them transferred to his Episcopal Palace at Winchester; an anachronistic forebear of Lord Carleton and Lord Elgin, he was considered by the Romans themselves to be a typically English eccentric.[35] And a Magister Gregorius from Oxford (ca. 1250), while going around Rome admiring and measuring classical buildings, fell in love with a Venus statue to the extent that its "magic persuasion" forced him to visit it time and again in spite of its considerable distance from his lodgings.[36]

VI.

In the domain of early Latin writing England also produced two strikingly contrastive phenomena neither of which, so far as I know, has a true parallel on the Continent. One of these phenomena consists of texts distinguished by violent passion and a deliberate obscurity which might invite comparison with the "chimerical darkness" of Lycophron's *Alexandra*, were it not for the fact that they represent an entirely different principle of obfuscation. The dark sayings of Lycophron's Cassandra are in reality entirely rational, condensed into correct iambic trimeters, couched in somewhat mannered but perfectly normal language, and made obscure and oracular only by the excessive use of erudite circumlocution—as if a modern author were to inform us of the fact that Mozart was born at Salzburg in 1756, when Frederick the Great started the Seven Years' War, by telling us that the Lord of Peace took up the sword when Orpheus reappeared in a castle of salt. The opposite is true of such seventh-century effusions as the *Hisperica Famina* or the *Description of Ireland* inserted at the beginning of Jonas of Bobbio's *Life of St. Colombanus*.[37]

Here the subject matter consists of intensely real, subjective experiences. The *Hisperica Famina* describes a ferocious disputation of great scholars, a bloody fight in which the author himself plays a heroic role, a day in school beginning with an impressive depiction of the awakening of life in the early morning, a shipwreck, etc.; the *Description of Ireland* is devoted solely to the dangers and the beauty of the Irish sea with its breathtaking sunrises and sunsets. And the obscurity of these texts results entirely from the violence of emotion; the eccentricity of speech and sound; the boldness of the imagery; the untamed power of the rhythm—a kind of rhapsodic prose in the *Famina*, free meters vaguely reminiscent of the hexameter in the *Description of Ireland*; the disjointed grammar; and, above all, the fiery bombast of a language which intermixes Latin with Greek, "Hisperic" and freely invented words. Even in a translation, which must render all these outlandish words by normal English ones, the effect is extraordinary; in the original Latin, it is simply stupendous: "This island," it says in the poem inserted into the Life of St. Columbanus,

> awaits the setting of the Titan [viz., the sun god] while the world turns and light descends into the western shadows—the sea, with its measureless masses of waves, abysses horrible in color, a profusion of hair curling everywhere. White, glistening robe (*peplo kana*), broad backs of blue, smiting man's hiding places on the foaming shore, the farthest bay on earth. Never suffer the shores we know so well to be entrusted with a gentle ship that craves the quivering brine. Over such lands does tawny Titan descend at the dense light of Arcturus and moves, revolving, to other parts of the world. Following the north wind, he strives for his rising in the east, that born to new life he may restore the kindly light to the world and scatter his fire far and wide over the trembling sky. And so, reaching all the goal posts of day and night in his course, he illumines the earth with his brightness and makes the world lovely, dripping with heat.

It is almost impossible to read this early poem without thinking of Ossian and William Turner and without remembering the famous definition of the "sublime" penned by John Dennis in 1693: "The sense of all this (viz., a dangerous and beautiful journey through the Alps) produc'd different motions in me, viz., a delightful Horrour, a terrible Joy, and at the same time that I was infinitely pleas'd, I trembled."[38] We are confronted with an anticipation of genuine English "romanticism" by a thousand years.

And yet, the very period which produced this glorious piece of imagistic poetry yielded to an impulse as unromantic as possible: an almost obsessive interest in classical prosody. "The Anglo-Saxons," writes Raby, "seem to have had a preoccupation with meter in its mechanical aspects"; even within the framework of their own poems they "liked to describe the meter they were using."[39] Precisely such authors as St. Columba or Aldhelm of Malmesbury, who often indulged in an exuberant obscurity reminiscent of the *Hisperica Famina* and the *Description of Ireland,* do not forget to inform their readers of the meter employed—whether *versus bipedales*[40] or carefully constructed hexameters.[41] And while a Continental writer of the seventh century such as Virgil of Toulouse (fl. ca. 630?) betrays a truly abysmal ignorance of classical versification,[42] Bede's only slightly later *De arte metrica* is an expert and utterly reasonable introduction to classical prosody, correctly defining the various classical meters yet accepting rhythm (*modulatio sine ratione*) as even more important than meter pure and simple (*modulatio cum ratione*), which enjoyed a well-deserved reputation for centuries.[43]

VII.

This English duality is especially evident in those mediaeval texts which record, or purport to record, impressions of works of art in purely descriptive fashion. It has been said that English sources of this kind, particularly of the twelfth century, are "characterized by a far more vivid description" than are their continental parallels.[44] This statement is very true but may be susceptible of specification.

In the first place, texts of this kind, whether in prose or verse, evince a surprising ability—promoted, perhaps, by the very insularity of a civilization looking to both Celtic Ireland and the Roman or Romanized Continent—to make stylistic distinctions and analyses at times anticipating the efforts of the modern art historian.

A continental chronicler of the thirteenth century could characterize the difference between the Early-Romanesque west part and the Gothic nave of a German church (St. Peter's at Wimpfen im Tal, fig. 16) only by stating that the latter was built "in the French manner" (*opere Francigeno*), that its windows and piers "followed the English fashion" (*ad instar Anglici operis*) and that it was constructed of "ashlars" (*sectis lapidibus*) rather than rough stones.[45] Gervase of Canterbury, writing nearly a hundred years earlier and describing the choir of Canterbury Cathedral rebuilt by William of Sens after the famous conflagration of 1174, goes out of his way to provide a thorough analysis of "the difference between the old structure and the new" (*quae sit operis utriusque differentia*) which amounts to a definition of the Gothic style as opposed to the Romanesque. He comes up with such distinctions as that between groin vaults and vaults provided with ribs and keystones (*fornices planae, fornices arcuatae et clavatae*), or that between stone carvings "looking as if they had been done with an axe rather than a chisel" (*utpote sculpta secure et non scisello*) and "subtle and competent sculpture" (*sculptura subtilis* and *sculptura idonea*). And at one point he even surprisingly anticipates Paul Frankl's distinction between the Romanesque and Gothic styles as "additive" and "divisive" in stating that in the old structure the transepts were separated from the choir by high walls, whereas in the new "the transepts, not separated from the choir by any intervening feature (*interstitio*), appeared to convene in one keystone in the middle of the big vault which surmounts the four principal piers" (fig. 17).[46]

If Osbert de Clare, Henry of Blois, and Magister Gregorius could fall in love with classical statuary, Giraldus Cambrensis, writing at the beginning of the thirteenth century, could do justice to the style of an ancient Irish manuscript believed to have been produced for St. Bridget in miraculous fashion; his words sound like a modern art historian's description of, say, the *Book of Kells* (fig. 18):

> This book contains the Four Gospels according to the Concordance of St. Jerome; and there are about as many different illustrations, distinguished by various colors, as there are pages. Here you may see the face of the All-Highest divinely expressed; there the mystical figures of the Evangelists, now having six wings, nor four, now two; here the eagle, there the calf; here the face of a man, there that of a lion; and other figures almost infinite in number. When you consider these pictures in a superficial and ordinary manner they will appear as blots rather than coherent shapes (*litura potius quam ligatura*), and you will fail to perceive any subtlety where there

is nothing but subtlety. But when you concentrate the visual power of your eyes upon a more thorough examination, and with a sustained effort penetrate the secrets of art, you will be able to perceive intricacies so delicate and subtle, so close-knit and involved, so knotted and interlaced, and so much illumined by colors which have preserved their freshness up to our day, that you will attribute the composition of all this to the industry of angels rather than humans (*tam delicatas et subtiles, tam arctas et artitas, tam nodosas et vinculatim colligatas, tamque recentibus adhuc coloribus illustratas notare poteris intricaturas, ut vero haec omnia potius angelica quam humana diligentia iam asseveraris esse composita*).[47]

In the second place, the texts in question are indeed distinguished by a stupendous richness in technical detail and a certain preoccupation with measurements comparable to the early Anglo-Saxon interest in prosody: the height of the church tower at Wilton, said to surpass the buildings of Babylon and Rome, is later on determined as amounting to exactly 120 cubits,[48] and when a thirteenth-century converse brother of Melrose Abbey describes the curious behavior of the moon—which he had observed to split in half, to transform itself into a crenelated castle and subsequently into an "elegant ship," then to change back to a castle, and finally to return to normal—he does not fail to mention that the distance between the two halves amounted to about one "stadium" and that the castle displayed a royal banner whose little streamers (*lingulae sive caudulae*) were fluttering in the breeze.[49] There is, however, on the other hand a marked tendency to subjectivize the phenomena on a purely psychological plane, more often than not by way of what is known as "empathy." After its many transformations, the moon strikes the good Frater of Melrose as having "suffered an injury so as to remain disturbed, dejected and distressed, pale and discolored" (*quasi iniuria passa, turbata, contristata et conturbata, pallida mansit et decolorata*). In the versified *Life of St. Hugh of Lincoln* the carefully joined and smoothed walls of the choir and transept of Lincoln Cathedral (rebuilt by St. Hugh between 1192 and 1220) "despise" the idea of being composed of individual stones and "feign to consist of a continuous matter, to be a work of nature rather than art, to be a unity rather than a union"; and the disengaged colonnettes surrounding the octagonal piers "seem to perform a solemn dance."[50]

Light is, therefore, hardly ever interpreted—as, for example, by Suger of St.-Denis—as a metaphysical principle; it tends to be accepted as a purely natural phenomenon (we may remember that three of the four great

fig. 16. Church of St. Peter, Wimpfen im Tal. Bildarchiv Foto Marburg.

fig. 17.   Cathedral of Canterbury, choir, looking east. London, Courtauld Institute of Art.

fig. 18.   Book of Kells, folio 34, Trinity College Library, Dublin.
Berlin, Archiv für Kunst und Geschichte.

mediaeval representatives of optics, Roger Bacon, John Peckham, and Robert Grosseteste, were Englishmen) conducive, however, to a distinctly subjective, aesthetic experience. In the description of the church at Wilton, the rays of the sun penetrate the church "through sheer glass and pure sapphire" (a precious dark blue glass which, at the time, had to be imported from the East), and "golden light strikes the faces of the people when they enter so that all things seem to rejoice in the rays of the reflected sun."[51] The walls of the choir of Lincoln Catheral, just mentioned, seem to consist of a nonporous matter glistening like the star-studded firmament (*Non tot laxa poris sed crebro sidere fulgens*) while the surfaces of its "dancing" colonnettes, "more highly polished than a newly grown finger nail, oppose the bright stars to the reflected rays of vision" (*Exterior facies, nascente politior ungue, / Clara repercussis opponit visibus astra*).[52]

This brings us to the third and most important point: the visual experiences described in this and other texts tend to anticipate, to an astonishing degree—and in a manner unknown on the Continent—the specifically "romantic" preoccupation with infinity and night.

That the polished surface of the Lincoln colonnettes "oppose the bright stars to the reflected rays of vision" seems to suggest a nocturnal visit. And what is here only implied, is explicitly stated in Wulfstan's remarkable description of Winchester Cathedral rebuilt by Bishop Elphegus (reigned 984–1005). Like Gervase of Canterbury, Wulfstan (whose poem is addressed to Bishop Elphegus himself) is very accurate and circumstantial, down to a minute description of the gigantic organ which had to be played by two organists while seventy strong men, "dripping with sweat," worked its twenty-six bellows. But he praises the east tower—paying a special tribute to the gilded weather cock which "nobly governs the transient empire and, turning ceaselessly, faces the rain-carrying winds from all directions and bravely suffers the impact of the horrid-sounding whirlwind, storms and snow"—not only because of its height but also because the windows that pierce its five storeys open up a panoramic view "over the four quarters of the earth" (*Quinque tenet patulis segmenta oculata fenestris / Per quadrasque plagas pandit ubique vias*). And the most amazing feature of his poem is an evocation of the impression produced by the church at night when the moon rises and the stars are out:

> On top [of the roof] there is a crest arrangement with gilded globes, and a golden radiance embellishes the whole work. Whenever the moon shines

fig. 19. Rolls-Royce automobile. Crewe, Cheshire, Rolls Royce Motor Cars Ltd.

fig. 20. Charles Sykes, R. A., the "Silver Lady" on the Rolls-Royce radiator. Bildarchiv Frankfurter Allgemeine Zeitung.

at its glorious rise, another radiance soars from the sacred structure to the celestial bodies; when a wanderer, passing by, observes [the church] by night, he believes that the earth, too, has its stars.[53]

Even Gervase of Canterbury, though expressing himself in prose rather than in well-constructed elegiac couplets, is not impervious to romantic sensations. Having described the origin and hidden progress of the fire of 1174—and so minute is his description that we obtain a clear picture of the old choir's roof construction—as well as the desperate efforts of monks and laymen to get it under control, he goes on to say that the wooden choir stalls were ignited by burning fragments of the rafters and that in the end the whole "glorious structure" went up in flames which, "multiplied by so big a mass of wood," reached up to fifteen cubits. But while he depicts the witnesses to this spectacle as tearing their hair and hitting the wall with their heads, he calls the spectacle itself *mirabile, immo miserabile*—"wonderful though pitiful."[54] Here again, we have, more than five centuries before John Dennis, a clear anticipation of that basic "romantic" experience: "A delightful Horrour, a terrible Joy."

These, then, are what I have facetiously called the ideological antecedents of the Rolls-Royce radiator (fig. 19). The composition of this radiator sums up, as it were, twelve centuries of Anglo-Saxon preoccupations and aptitudes: it conceals an admirable piece of engineering behind a majestic Palladian temple front; but this Palladian temple front is surmounted by the wind-blown "Silver Lady" in whom *art nouveau* appears infused with the spirit of unmitigated "romanticism." The radiator and the radiator cap have not been changed since the first Rolls-Royce car was delivered at the beginning of 1905; the "Silver Lady," modeled by Charles Sykes, R. A., was added as early as 1911 (fig. 20).[55] Since then the "face" of the Rolls-Royce has remained unaltered: it has continued to reflect the essence of the British character for more than half a century. May it never be changed!

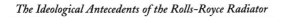

Erwin Panofsky: A Curriculum Vitae

Hannover, 30 March 1892—Princeton, 14 March 1968

William S. Heckscher

In our minds Erwin Panofsky is very much alive. Yet it is my task this afternoon to speak to you at a symposium arranged by the Department of Art and Archaeology in conjunction with the Art Museum and the Library of Princeton University to honor and commemorate the man whose life on earth has been concluded.

If I were to choose a motto for my address, it would—almost inevitably—have to be *De mortuis nil nisi bene*. As I ask myself how Erwin Panofsky would react to this choice of motto, I can hear his voice saying, "But, Bill, that doesn't mean that you have to confine yourself only to good things in speaking about me; if that were the case, we would have to say *De mortuis nil nisi bonum*. The adverb *bene* in this context simply means, 'Speak of the dead only in a just and proper manner.'"

Already a considerable body of biographical and memorial essays has been published by friends and disciples. With the generous help of Gerda Panofsky I have, I think, read most of them. Panofsky's friends—Rens and Stella Lee, Harold and Ruth Cherniss, Emma Epps, Walter Mosse, Dave Coffin, John Rupert Martin, Margot Einstein, Jan Bialostocki, Carl Nordenfalk, Edward Lowinsky, Roger d'Hulst, Martin Davies, and others—have obliged me by talking to me about their recollections. As I listened to their voices it became abundantly clear to me that Erwin Panofsky's image changes from biographer to biographer—a true sign of the immense vitality with which he impressed people near and far. I trust that for this very reason all of you will understand why the curriculum vitae which I shall sketch here may not entirely agree with your own impressions of Panofsky the man and the scholar. Whatever its deficiencies, my account is the nearest I could come to the historical truth by fulfilling my task highly selectively and yet, as I hope, in a just and proper manner.

I wish to record my gratitude to Gerda Panofsky for giving permission to quote from her late husband's letters and other written communications. I am particularly grateful to the following who have assisted me with information of various kinds and who have obliged me deeply by critical readings of my manuscript in various stages: Mrs. Cameron F. Bunker, Mrs. Virginia W. Callahan, David R. Coffin, Martin Davies, Roger A. d'Hulst, Warren Kirkendale, Mrs. Hedy Backlin-Landman, Emanuel Winternitz. Above all I wish to thank my friend H. W. Janson for having read my manuscript with critical attention.

I have often wondered why Erwin Panofsky never considered writing his own memoirs. He may have felt that a good deal of autobiographical material was deposited in his other writings. Be that as it may, he has left to his friends and critics the task of tracing the fascinating phenomenon of a life that in its spiritual and intellectual growth went through Protean changes and yet remained ever true to the ideals of humanism from beginning to end.

Panofsky's work, although based on genuine respect for the achievement of others—above all a wholly justified veneration of his teachers, along with a deep awareness of tradition—was nevertheless revolutionary in character. It is no exaggeration to state that almost every single one of his publications influenced the development and, more often than not, determined the direction of his chosen discipline, the history of art. He pursued his work with undiminished gusto through no less than fifty-five creative years. Conservative and radical at the same time, his oeuvre faithfully mirrors the growth of art history as a scholarly discipline. The bibliography of Panofsky's publications makes us marvel at the bold imagination with which he tackled ever new fields. Yet, strange as it may seem, a student of his *Nachlass* cannot escape the impression that the publications are no more than the part of the iceberg that emerges from the water. Panofsky left a vast number of unfinished projects in various stages of completion. There are countless notes arranged by title; his personal copies of art historical reference works and monographs crowded with elaborate marginal commentaries, diagrams, and sketches; there are the manuscripts of lectures, some in the form of syllabi, among them detailed libretti of university courses dealing with the Baroque on either side of the Alps and with problems in sculpture, painting, and architecture of all periods; tangible plans to deal with Michelangelo and Bernini problems; a study of many years, done jointly with Dora Panofsky, of Poussin's *Flight into Egypt*; promising suggestions on the mysterious Voynich manuscript; and, possibly the most intriguing problem of all, an in many ways radically new interpretation of the musician angels in the Ghent Altarpiece—the "Glee Club," as he called them—a sharp veering away from his own cherished earlier concepts, necessitated by Coremans' technical observations-in-depth. Panofsky, it seems, confided these conclusions only to a small and ever shrinking circle of *proximi* who had taken part in the Brussels *Colloquium doctum* of 1954.[1]

Then there are his letters. Their range and number remind us of the splendid *epistolarium* left by Erasmus of Rotterdam. Not unlike Erasmus's, Panofsky's letters were circulated among close friends for edification and instruction. Lucky those whose names were on this mailing-list!

In addition, Panofsky wrote occasional verse, serious and satirical epigrams, sonnets, and limericks, composed with prosodic finesse in German, English, Latin, French, and Greek.

Last but not least he will be remembered for his obiter dicta, treated by himself and, alas, by most of his friends as mere ephemera. Their range was enormous. What made them so arresting is that often they would touch upon areas of the history of art not mentioned in Panofsky's publications or lectures. He spoke, for example, of Modigliani (who of all modern artists was nearest to him) as one "who had produced the kind of human beings that are a race by themselves—very much like Michelangelo." He was fascinated by Mondrian, whom he called "slave of the square on which he worked, and that is to say slave of his self-imposed restrictions." Doughnuts, Emmenthaler, and Henry Moore all shared a common element, "the activation of holes in matter." He disliked "unreliable" people. Of William Blake he said, "I can't stand him. I don't mind if a man is really mad, like Hölderlin. True madness may yield poetical flowers. But I don't like mad geniuses walking all the time at the brink of an abyss. Blake is all negative and unreliable." Van Gogh was to him "a genius without talent." A whole evening of Marcel Marceau, charming in small measure, was "just as bad as a Chinese poem of thirty-four syllables on the Prune Blossom or a sonata on the G-string that lasts two hours."

Panofsky heard words and entire sentences in his dreams and he had what he called visions—verbal continuations of his dreams in a half-waking state. Once he dreamt of an ugly old lady and woke up with the untranslatable phrase, "Zum Schauen bestellt." Rainer Maria Rilke appeared to him as a "mail order Don Juan." He told how "in my dream I went to the Princeton Inn and saw the late lamented Albert Friend, looking very rosy and self-satisfied, sitting in the corner of one of the big davenports there. He beckoned to me and asked me to sit down beside him, which I did, opening the conversation with the words, 'Well, Bert, how is it in Hell?' Whereupon he answered, 'I *like* it there.'" In another dream he saw a hermit outside his cave, beating his breast with a stone, while out of the mouth of the cave came a scroll inscribed with the words, "Long distance for you, Sir."

Erwin Panofsky was to his last breath a magician with words and he was, increasingly, conscious of their seminal power. At the same time he was, like few of his colleagues, "begotten to see." Critically and lovingly he observed the world from the much maligned "Ivory Tower" [Bibl. 116*].[2] Seeing and recording what he saw were to him the most gratifying intellectual activities. In the last hours of his life—his features more than ever resembling those of the aging, owl-eyed Voltaire—he held, with his arms stretched above his head, the ponderous plate volume of Millard Meiss's *French Painting in the Time of the Duc de Berry*. Calling the attention of his visitor, Harold Cherniss, to the miniature showing Marcia portraying herself with the aid of a mirror, he pointed out that this was one of the earliest manifestations of a self-portrait in the making and cited with flawless precision the particulars of the manuscript in the Bibliothèque Nationale—fr. 12420, fol. 100 v.

It was this unique combination of near-perfect visual and verbal retention that enabled Panofsky to "write" whole chapters of books-yet-to-come without committing a single word to paper. He could effortlessly recite such unwritten chapters to the breathless companion who tried to keep up with him and his dog Jerry on a brisk walk through the tangled woods behind the Institute for Advanced Study; since I was the companion, I might record one of his rare mnemonic lapses. After the walk I left Princeton for about two weeks. On my return we resumed our walks, and Panofsky, who had forgotten that he had quoted paragraph after paragraph from his not-yet-written *Galileo* [Bibl. 117] to me earlier, repeated the identical passages—words, commas, and all.

Walter Friedlaender, one of Panofsky's teachers and a lifelong friend, related how to Erwin Panofsky's cradle in Hannover there hurried two fairies, Wealth and Intelligence. The third, Good Looks, didn't make it. In her stead came a fairy who said, "Whichever book you open, you will find precisely the passage you need." Adolph Goldschmidt is said to have remarked of his student, "Wenn Erwin ein Bild sieht, dann fällt ihm immer gleich was ein."

---

*The numbers in brackets hereinafter correspond to those in the bibliography of Panofsky's publications cited below, n. 3, p. 199; the full references are given on pp. 194–95.—Ed.

fig. 1.   Erwin Panofsky with his first wife Frau Dora, in front of his house in Princeton, 1956.
Princeton, Dr. Gerda Panofsky.

This well-attested serendipity, however legendary its origins, served Panofsky throughout his life. His astonishingly rare and brief visits to libraries reminded the discreet observer of the behavior of an ecstatic insect in quest of honey, nervously flitting from flower to flower, sampling here and there, until it comes to rest on the preordained blossom, imbibing the nectar with deep absorption. Witty and incisive, skeptical and warmhearted, possessed of limitless curiosity ("Do you know the address of the Swiss Museum of Baby Shoes?"), yet on the whole as discreet as most eloquent people with a natural urge to communicate, Panofsky knew how to guard his creative moments with great stubbornness when faced by what he considered trivial outside interference. He said of himself (November 1946), "Every six weeks I have a thought. The rest of the time I work." There was nothing of the scholar's mock humility in such reflections.

Panofsky has given us a nostalgic description of his school years in Berlin at the Joachimsthalsche Gymnasium [Bibl. 116]. His high school teachers were scholars first and foremost. At the age of sixteen he knew Dante's *Divine Comedy* by heart. He attributed this feat, as well as his fluent command of Italian, to the unconventional method of Gino Ravaili. This gifted teacher, scorning the use of grammar, syntax, and vocabulary, began with the text right away. Young Panofsky also committed to memory all of Shakespeare's sonnets and the themes of the preludes and fugues of Bach's *Well-Tempered Clavier.*

A disciple of two giants in his field, Adolph Goldschmidt and Wilhelm Vöge, Panofsky received his doctorate at Freilburg in 1914 with a dissertation on Dürer's art theory [Bibl. 1, 2]. Prior to this he had been awarded the coveted prize of the Grimm-Stiftung of Berlin University for a brilliant study of the Italian-inspired mathematics in Dürer's work. Thus at the age of eighteen Panofsky not only anticipated his magnum opus, the two-volume *Albrecht Dürer* [Bibl. 84], but also his revolutionary mathematics-based studies on the theory of proportion [Bibl. 14], on perspective as a "symbolic form" [Bibl. 36], and, ultimately, on Dürer as a mathematician.[3]

In 1916 he married Dora Mosse, whom he had met when both attended a Goldschmidt seminar in Berlin. Dora, older by eight years, preceded her husband in death. She was one of his severest, most perceptive, and also most stimulating critics. For decades she keenly felt herself to be living in the shadow of Erwin Panofsky's mental superiority. Yet at the age of sixty, after a severe illness, she unexpectedly found herself as a scholar, able to create independently of her husband's immediate interests. It was this miraculously gained self-reliance that enabled her to produce her remarkable work and to contribute an equal share to their joint endeavors: *Pandora's Box* [Bibl. 122] and "The Galérie François Ier at Fontainebleau" [Bibl. 129], two works in which Panofsky himself took special pride. In a letter of April 1958 he reported in his typical fashion, "The Swedish book (*Renaissance and Renascences*) [Bibl. 134] is ready but extremely bad; the Fontainebleau article is also ready and much better. The hardest thing I have to do is an introduction to Vöge's collected essays which I have to write in German and in such a way that it brings out some of his personality and makes my great affection for him apparent while avoiding the Thomas Mann type of obituary which begins with a brief description of the situation in which he met the deceased and then talks only about Thomas Mann."

If in retrospect we try to assess the influences, academic and personal, that shaped Erwin Panofsky's mind, I think we must beware of seeing him as a man nurtured by the "great books" or by the words of the "great masters" only. On the contrary, it was the curriculum-shunned texts, often written in a language either intentionally obscure or outright abstruse, that he taught us to appreciate as true supports of our humanistic studies. "Who has read *Hisperica famina?*" he might ask members of his privatissimum. "Are you familiar with Lycophron's *Alexandra?* Do you understand the significance of Virgilius Maro Grammaticus? Of Hiob Ludolph's Assyrian studies? Of Kepler's *Somnium?*" And when we shook our heads, he might add, "Gentlemen, you have yet to discover the value of useless knowledge." Some of us took heed and worked on obscure authors and sources, and did our best to acquire linguistic skills beyond what might be considered our call of duty. Hugo Buchthal, Adolf Katzenellenbogen, Lise Lotte Möller, H. W. Janson, Hanns Swarzenski, Walter Horn, Lotte Brand Philip, Hans Konrad Röthel, Peter Heinz von Blanckenhagen, Peter Hirschfeld (to mention only a few of Panofsky's students and disciples of Hamburg days), all indeed distinguished scholars in their own right, have successfully carried on and developed, often in ways quite remote from those of their great teacher, this Panofskian blend of the humanist tradition. Readers of his facetiously titled "The Ideological Antecedents of the Rolls-Royce Radiator" [Bibl. 155] will remember the significant role of *Hisperica famina* as a mythical predecessor "by a thousand years" of both Ossian and William Turner—and, we might add, James Joyce.[4]

However, we must not conclude from his undeniable delight in rariora, arcana, and aenigmatica in art and literature that Panofsky attached little significance to questions of aesthetic value or relative degree of historical importance. His mind saw itself incessantly challenged by the great in art. He contributed fundamental studies on Michelangelo and Leonardo, Albrecht Dürer and Piero di Cosimo, on Titian, Correggio, Bernini, and Poussin, on medieval sculpture and architecture, and on the great masters of the Northern Renaissance.

Hand in hand with a keen interest in aesthetic matters—not to be confused with the abhorred "appreciationism," which in his words "deprives naiveté of its charm without correcting its errors"—went Panofsky's doubts regarding aesthetics as a fruitful or even legitimate field of academic research. When asked to recommend a fundamental work on aesthetics, he would suggest to his students Jean Paul's *Vorschule der Aesthetik,* written about 1804, which he said not so long ago, is "infinitely better than Suzanne Langer."[5]

How had Panofsky come to discover Jean Paul? As a young man he was vacationing at Titisee, waiting for snow to come. As he waited, he opened at random Jean Paul's *Flegeljahre,* the great fragment of a novel that had grown out of the *Vorshule,* and read, "Jetzt brannte und zitterte in zartem Umriss eine Obstallée durchsichtig und riesenhaft in der Abendglut." He became a lifelong devotee of Germany's greatest and least appreciated prose writer.

A strong and lasting personal influence was exerted on the young student by the now forgotten Viktor Lowinsky, who wrote among other things "Raum und Geschehnis in Poussins Kunst," a study which appeared in Vol. XI of the *Zeitschrift für Aesthetik und allgemeine Kunstwissenschaft.* It might be termed a philosophical extension of Walter Friedlaender's monograph on Poussin. Panofsky described him as "the cleverest man I think I have ever met . . . a terribly witty man . . . a polyhistor . . . infinitely more attractive than the whole Stefan George circle." As late as January 1961 he sent me a Xerox copy of Lowinsky's "Poussin" which he had inscribed, "For 1914 or so, this is still a very good article! Pan." In reading it one senses the source of inspiration for the young Panofsky's highly formalized and encap-

fig. 2. Erwin Panofsky in his Hamburg study, 1920s.

sulated style of presentation, which permeated his Hamburg lectures on the Italian Baroque and on Dürer. The Lowinsky phase culminated in Panofsky's *Idea* of 1924 [Bibl. 24], a study of the theory of art from Plato to the seventeenth century, more philosophical than art-historical in character. When not so long ago I told Panofsky what *Idea* had meant to his students as a source of agony and frustration, he smiled and asked, "Eine Kater-Idee?" [6]

Being a man of independent means, the young doctor of philosophy planned to lead the life of a free-lance scholar doing research in the pursuit of art-historical problems. However, no sooner had the inflation of the German *Mark* after the First World War deprived him and his family of their fortune than the newly founded University of Hamburg offered him, in 1921, the chair of art history with the initial rank of *Privatdozent*. Five years later he was made professor. Hamburg's *Kunsthistorisches Seminar*, as the department was called, soon attracted young and highly promising scholars as teachers. Edgar Wind, Hans Liebeschütz, Charles de Tolnay became, each in a different way, associates of Panofsky. Gustav Pauli ("the incarnation of Hanseatic *noblesse*"), the farsighted director of the Kunsthalle who had proposed Panofsky for his university post, regarded and treated him from the outset as *collega proximus*. At the same time Aby Warburg, Fritz Saxl, Rudolf Wittkower, and Gertrud Bing of the Kulturwissenschaftliche Bibliothek Warburg linked up with Panofsky's "seminar" in an informal fashion. The international frame of this research group rested on a series of published lectures, the Warburg *Vorträge*, and a series of monographic *Studien*, as well as the now little-known analytical bibliography devoted to themes and motifs of classical antiquity in postclassical times. Above them all, however, towered the personality of Ernst Cassirer, "the only German philosopher of our generation who to the cultured was a substitute for the Church—when you were in love or otherwise unhappy" (November 1946).

Panofsky's public university lectures attracted audiences of several hundred. They were profound, eloquent, and of a cogency that remarkably anticipated his American style of writing and speaking. One wonders what part the rhetorician and philosopher Edgar Wind may have played in the shaping of Panofsky at this time. Wind, who had spent some time in America, brought to his work and to his ravishing style of lecturing a lucidity and a deceptive simplicity that filled academically trained Germans with noticeable *Unbeha-*

gen. He has described to me his first encounters with Panofsky: "I had not yet met Panofsky at that time. When I wrote him my first letter, to enquire whether I could study with him, he was not yet 'habilitated' but he took me on—at the advice of the university—in a private capacity, to await consummation after his inaugural lecture. So I had the rare privilege of listening to the *Probevorlesung* of my instructor. It was a highly dialectical exercise, a comparison of Leonardo da Vinci and Michelangelo as artistic types, in which the antitheses exploded like firecrackers . . . Panofsky had in those days a distinctly romantic physiognomy. A thick moustache (almost Nietzschean) covered his upper lip, and long whiskers descended in front of his ears, throwing into prominence the luminous eyes and the high forehead over which the black hair was pretty long though already receding. His face, believe it or not, was rather thin, and his expression always pensive. On the day when he was to examine me for the doctor's degree (29 July 1922), we met accidentally in the street, since we were both walking toward the same destination. We had a long and funny conversation, but as we approached the university building, he suddenly felt that our intimacy might be regarded as unbecoming in official quarters. So he suggested that I should go in first, while he would walk around the building. On his arrival he greeted me as if he had never seen me in his life, and then continued, for an hour, the conversation we had begun in the street."[7]

Above all it was in those years our good fortune to observe our teacher at close quarters. He grew by leaps and bounds, with every lecture course and with every new publication. We waylaid him after his lectures and frequently went with him to his hospitable apartment in the Alte Rabenstrasse, debating, discussing, reciting—often until the dawn of the following day. Panofsky's self-created setting, the "Hamburg Seminar," was remarkable among art-historical centers in Europe for what might be called its cultural ecology. It was cradled between Kunsthalle and Warburg Library. Its wider framework was a curiously sober and mercurial Biedermeier city, a *Freie und Hansestadt* which, even though its leading citizens tended to mistrust the Muses, stood nevertheless uniquely open to the intellectual currents radiating from the British Isles and from across the Atlantic.

In the unquestionably glorious years of the Weimar Republic, Erwin Panofsky laid the foundation of his fame as a scholar who helped to change the

fig. 3. Erwin Panofsky with William Sebastian Heckscher in Princeton, 1950s.

aesthetic and antiquarian orientation of art history and to turn it into a humanistic discipline which boldly ventured into adjacent fields but without relinquishing the traditional methods practiced by connoisseurs ("laconic art historians") and art historians ("loquacious connoisseurs"). Iconology, in the modern sense of the term, was first propounded on the eve of the First World War by Aby Warburg in a twenty-minute lecture at the International Art Historical Congress in Rome. The iconological method, we may say, reached its full flowering in Panofsky's wonderful surrealistic tour de force, *Herkules am Scheidewege,* which appeared in 1930 as one of the Warburg *Studien* [Bibl. 45].[8] It was about this time that the goddess Fortuna intervened, in the guise of Walter W. S. Cook of New York University, with unexpectedly favorable consequences. Two years before the enforced exodus of the intellectual élite that followed the advent of Hitler, Panofsky became a regular guest professor in the United States, at the invitation of Professor Cook.* He lectured in the basement of the Metropolitan Museum of Art under the auspices of what was to become the Institute of Fine Arts, New York University's graduate department of art history, and immediately made a deep impression on his American colleagues and students. On his first arrival, in September 1931, he was met and welcomed at the pier by Millard Meiss, whom Cook had dispatched as his emissary and who was assigned to him as an assistant for the term. Meiss, who also lectured at the institute, was then working toward his Ph.D. degree. In the customs shed the discussion almost immediately turned to the art at the court of the Duc de Berry, a subject to which Meiss brought a thorough knowledge of the trecento. We may say that what started as a casual conversation among two young scholars ripened into the monumental work whose growth and final fruition Panofsky was happy to witness.

In 1933 Erwin Panofsky presented what may be termed his American calling-card: the long article, "Classical Mythology in Medieval Art," which was published in *Metropolitan Museum Studies* [Bibl. 56]. He had written it in collaboration with Fritz Saxl, following their joint effort, *Melencolia I,* of ten years before. Although addressed to an English-speaking public, it was conceived in the highly polished, antithetically grouped phrases so characteristic of Panofsky's mature Hamburg style. His statements were clear,

---

*Evidently it was Richard Offner, then chairman of the graduate section of fine arts at New York University, who sponsored Panofsky's visits to America (cf. Smyth, as in n. 13, pp. 202–3).—Ed.

logical, and highly didactic. With Panofsky-Saxl's "Classical Mythology," the Warburgian preoccupation with the *Nachleben* of paganism—the transformation of classical mythology in post-classical times—made its entry into the world of American humanistic scholarship.

Providentially, Panofsky escaped from Nazi Germany unscathed. He joined the professorial ranks of Abraham Flexner's newly founded Institute for Advanced Study at Princeton as the first permanent member of its School of Historical Studies. At the same time, he established and further cemented his affiliations with New York University and Princeton University. His influence on generation after generation of American graduate students in art history was immense.[9] One of his earliest students at Princeton, John Rupert Martin, referred to the "transfiguring and illuminating quality of Panofsky's teaching, which was farthest removed from archaeology." It was Panofsky's unconventional approach that "made his tough seminars so exciting from the very beginning, as when, discussing the International Style, he would start by reading the poetry by Charles d'Orléans, comparing him to Verlaine—and doing all this, needless to say, in French." Panofsky was indeed, as Martin suggests, antagonistic to what he himself called "the naive aspects of the strictly archaeological method." After a lecture on the wells of Periclean Athens, he was heard to murmur, "Well, well, well." One of his dearest friends in Princeton, Erik Sjöqvist, told me: "When Pan discovered that I considered the humanistic and historical interpretation of our material as the only really important thing, he at once asked me, 'If so, why did you became an archaeologist?'" (letter of September 16, 1968).

A "transplanted European" [Bibl. 115] Panofsky elicited in America, as a scholar and as a man, a deeper and even more enduring response than he had in Germany. It is characteristic of him that he never forgot his scholarly debt to the great men among the American art historians of his and the preceding generation: Charles Rufus Morey [Bibl. 120], Arthur Kingsley Porter, Baldwin Smith, Albert M. Friend, Meyer Schapiro, Fiske Kimball. Kimball, the great museum director, he placed beside Pauli of Hamburg and Carl Nordenfalk of Stockholm, who to him combined two indispensable qualities: they were true gentlemen, and they were superb administrators because they were scholars first and foremost. (Their very opposite in Panofsky's eyes was a man like Francis Henry Taylor, who to him was "a Sunday iconographer.") The great American art historians Panofsky regarded as living proof of the fact that the vogue of humanistic scholarship in America was not triggered by European immigrant professors; it originated, he liked to point out, soon after the First World War and experienced its first golden age in the decade 1923–33. At the same time he did not hide his genuine concern as he noted the undercurrents of barbarism and anti-intellectualism in America, favored and cultivated by the intellectual and political libertines who forever menace the very roots of cultural traditions and humane values [Bibl. 78, 116].

Princeton, with its circle of loyal friends and a constant stream of visiting scholars from all corners of the globe, had a dreamlike quality for Panofsky. A priority target for visitors from abroad, it was to him above all "Erewhon," and he called its university "the last Indian Reserve for gentlemen (because a gentleman is a gentleman only in a womanless atmosphere)" (1947). Although he described women as a predatory animals whose prey was time (*Zeitraubtiere*), Panofsky was far from ever being an outright gynophobe. He deeply respected great scholars such as Eleanor Marquand, Hetty Goldman, Dorothy Miner, Marjorie Nicholson, Mirella Levi d'Ancona, Lola Szladits, and Virginia W. Callahan. He admired and loved Rosalie B. Green, the learned director of the Index of Christian Art at Princeton University, who was to him a constant source of iconographic information pertaining to things medieval. He praised what he called her Euclidian ability to create *ex ungue leonem*. All this, however, did not keep him from remarking, in reference to the tireless labors of the exclusively female staff of the Princeton Index, "Parturiunt mures, nascitur ridiculus mons." Similarly, he admired Rosa Schapire in Hamburg. But when, in a lecture on her first visit to Greece, she confessed to having kissed the ground upon arrival, Panofsky could not refrain from whispering, "Er konnte sich ja nicht wehren!" (German *Boden* happens to be masculine.) Yet he felt the need to balance this remark by immediately adding Ovid's "Cadmus agit grates, peregrinaeque oscula terrae / Figit, et ignotos montes agrosque salutat." His gratitude to Roxanne Forster was deep and justified. To the last she was at his side as his secretary and friend with whom he battled over every cadence, every comma, from both a semantic and a phonetic point of view—often agonizingly but always to his and his readers' benefit.

Panofsky's book, *Studies in Iconology* (1939) [Bibl. 74], marks the turning point at which iconology ceased to be an ancillary discipline and became an indispensable part of art-historical method. The parade pieces were "Piero di Cosimo," "Father Time," "Blind Cupid," "The Neo-Platonic Movement." The introductory chapter of less than thirty pages, with its ingenious tables dissecting the three strata of subject matter and meaning, was to become the classic statement of iconographic and iconological procedure.[10] *Albrecht Dürer* [Bibl. 84], the first edition of which appeared at the Princeton University Press in 1943, is Panofsky's great and definitive tribute to the Nuremberg artist-humanist with whom his scholarly career had begun in 1911–12. It might also justly be called his answer to the Teutonic ideology of the Nazis, which, to the lasting detriment of German intellectual life, claimed to be able to distinguish between Germanic and Jewish scholarship.

On the morning of January 25, 1947, Panofsky received the invitation to give the Norton Lectures at Harvard University. He showed me the letter and, as I handed it back to him, he said with a wry smile, "Ach verflucht!" It was not until March 5 that he began writing. He commented in genuine despair, "I find nothing as difficult as starting." Six years later, ten years after the book on Dürer, the Norton Lectures appeared as a monumental publication under the title *Early Netherlandish Painting* [Bibl. 112]. Here his mastery of the English language had grown beyond mere virtuosity and had attained the level of a brilliantly sustained literary style, in perfect balance with the minutiae of the scholarly *apparatus criticus*.

Early Netherlandish Painting was preceded by two smaller books, both deeply revealing to the reader in quest of the author. I know that Panofsky passionately believed in the theses of *Gothic Architecture and Scholasticism* [Bibl. 106]. This work highlights, it seems to me, the specifically scholastic strain in his whole manner of thinking. He felt vulnerable in publishing this *confessio amantis*, more so than ever before or after. The other book, a critical edition of the Latin text, along with an impeccable translation, of the writings of Suger of Saint-Denis, is of particular interest because of its preface, a *New Yorker*-style "profile" of the great abbot [Bibl. 90]. It represents, mutatis mutandis, a spiritual autobiography of Panofsky himself.

The books just mentioned may justly be called a contribution to the history of ideas as much as to the history of art. Like most of Panofsky's subsequent publications, they began with the spoken word, as lectures or series of lectures. He knew how to preserve the character of the oral argument, even in his most formal writings. Panofsky acknowledged the momentous impact that the English language had had on the very foundations of his thinking and on his manner of presenting ideas in a lucid and organic, euphonious as well as logical way—so very different from the "woolen curtain" that so many Continental scholars, above all Germans and Dutch, interposed between themselves and their readers.

Erwin Panofsky was proud of the fact that he had one nearsighted and one farsighted eye: the best of two worlds. With Bernard Berenson in mind (he referred to him as "the art bishop of Florence") he remarked that connoisseurs as they get older become increasingly narrowminded and farsighted, while humanists become increasingly fairminded and nearsighted. The maturing process of Panofsky's mind did not lead to the all-too-common retreat of the aging scholar behind a parapet of profundities and generalities. Even by their intriguing and often intentionally bizarre titles, innumerable small but extremely significant articles attested his undiminished zest for venturing into ever new fields. We encounter, in the 1960s, essays such as *"Canopus Deus,* the Iconography of a Non-Existent God" [Bibl. 138]; "Homage to Fracastoro," on the role of syphilis in Renaissance art [Bibl. 141]; the revised dialogue, "Sokrates in Hamburg" [Bibl. 143]; "The Ideological Antecedents of the Rolls-Royce Radiator" [Bibl. 155]; "The Mouse that Michelangelo Failed to Carve" [Bibl. 161]; *"Sol Aequinoctialis Fuit Creatus. . . ,"* on Gregorian calendar reform [Bibl. 162], dedicated to his friend Alexandre Koyré; and his great book, all text and no footnotes: *Tomb Sculpture. Four Lectures on Its Changing Aspects from Ancient Egypt to Bernini* [Bibl. 160]; "the result of a somewhat morbid but rather intense interest in funerary art."[11]

In December 1959 I received a letter from Panofsky telling me that Millard Meiss had invited him ostensibly to a perfectly harmless luncheon at his house, "and when we entered the room we found ourselves confronted with major fragments of the committee that had clandestinely prepared what seems to be the most opulent *Festschrift* ever known to man . . . it is somewhat ironical that I shall receive the *Festschrift,* if I live that long, without being entitled to it. By this I mean not only that I am not worthy (that goes without saying) but also that the occasion for which the *Festschrift* was originally planned has now disappeared [Panofsky's retirement from the Institute had unexpectedly been postponed by two years] with the result that I find myself in the somewhat anomalous position of receiving a *Festschrift* without any obvious reason. I have a choice between either resigning before my time so as to justify the *Festschrift* or receiving the *Festschrift* with the feeling of a man who wakes up from apparent death in the middle of his own burial service, feeling somewhat sheepish and even a little indiscreet on account of having listened in on what was not really intended to be heard by himself." Some time after, early in 1960, Millard Meiss asked me to act for the editorial board and take the specially bound volumes of the *Festschrift* to their destination. Presenting them was not an easy task simply because Panofsky refused to put down Georges Wildenstein's *Paintings of Fragonard,* which he insisted on reading even after he had ushered me into his living room. The whole procedure was highly embarrassing for both of us. Finally, I repaired to the kitchen to mix us some drinks. Panofsky followed me, carrying the two heavy volumes, still in their slip case, and put them on the kitchen scales. Once the ice was broken, his delighted curiosity, especially regarding the "who's who" of the forty contributors, changed from astonishment to laughter, from laughter to frowning, and back to delighted laughter again.

The curriculum vitae of Erwin Panofsky would be wanting if no mention were made of at least some of his intellectual hobbies and idiosyncrasies. Here the movies rank, undoubtedly, in first place. Although his essay on the subject [Bibl. 64] has been reprinted more often than any of his other works, few professional film critics seem to have comprehended its message. It was only quite recently that it began to dawn on departments of art history and on the responsible deans that the history of the film represents the genesis and maturation of an art form which originated within living memory and which therefore can be analyzed in all its phases with almost clinical precision.[12] It was strangely touching to hear Panofsky discuss (on February 2, 1966) the enigmatic film by Alain Robbe-Grillet, *L'Année dernière á Marienbad,* which in 1961 had been filmed not there but at Nymphenburg and Schleissheim. As those who have seen the film will remember, the heroine, Delphine Seyrig, remains ambiguously uncertain whether or not she remembers what can only have been a love affair "last year at Marienbad." Panofsky said he was immediately reminded of Goethe, who at the age of seventy-four (Panofsky's own age at that point) had fallen in love with Ulrike von Levetzow, a girl in her late teens, whom he saw during three successive summers at Marienbad. The elements of Love, Death, and Oblivion in Goethe's commemorative poem, the *Marienbader Elegie,* seemed to Panofsky to anticipate the leitmotifs of the film. He noted the opening words of the elegy ("Was soll ich nun vom Wiedersehen hoffen. . . ?") and pointed out how the elements of clouded remembrance and erotic uncertainty were shared by both the poem and the film. He added that the director, Alain Resnais, had a way of leaving his actors uncommonly free to chart their own parts. Miss Seyrig might well have been familiar with Goethe's poem and its ambiguous message. Was she not, after all, the daughter of a famous and learned father, Henri Seyrig, archaeologist, former Directeur Général des Musées de France, and on repeated occasions a member of the Institute for Advanced Study at Princeton?[13]

Next to the film as an art form, Panofsky was fascinated by what he called the Aristotelian quality of the mystery or detective story. He liked to compare the Sherlock Holmes canon and its conscious or unconscious influence on all later writers of this genre to the importance that the canon of the Church Fathers held for the Middle Ages, "the assumption being that Sherlock Holmes' word was Truth. Discrepancies, as in the scholastic method, had to be ironed out." The Holmesian dictum that "if all that which is impossible has been excluded, the improbable that remains must be true," became in a half-serious way part of Panofsky's iconographic working method. He illustrated this by saying, "A saint receiving a rose from Heaven is improbable but convincing. If, on the other hand, Disraeli on entering Queen Victoria's drawing room finds the Queen smoking a big black cigar, this is possible but unconvincing and cannot therefore be admitted as a literary motif" (February 1948). One of Panofsky's favorites among crime story writers was Matthew Head (John Canaday), who reciprocated these feelings and inscribed *Another Man's Life,* "For E. P." On one occasion Matthew Head, Panofsky thought, had overstepped the limits of the mystery story. "The moment you inject psychology or rather psychopathology into a story of that kind," he said, "you take the onus of responsibility off the hero's shoulders. . . . A good detective or mystery story is, at present, the only category of literature where man *is* responsible—neither mother complex nor glandular disturbance can be used as an excuse . . . this genre represents the only relic of the pre-Freudian and the pre-Marxist past. *Roman psychologique* in the sense of Georges Simenon is acceptable; not, however, *roman pathologique.*"

Above all, perhaps, Panofsky was a devotee and a genuine connoisseur of music, in particular Mozart's. The Köchel *Verzeichnis* was one of the reference works he always had on hand. A distich—a dialogue between Posterity and Death—attests this great and reverent love:

> *Quare, Mors, juvenem Wolfgangum praeripuisti?*
> *ne secreta mea prodere pergat opus.*
> *(Why, oh death, hast thou abducted the youthful Wolfgang ahead of his time?*
> *I did this lest his work might continue giving away my secrets.)*

I believe I am right in describing Panofsky as a man swayed by deep emotions in all stages of his life. This was true despite his almost puritanical insistence on integrity and truthfulness in his utterances, private as well as public. He approached music, art, and literature both intellectually and emotionally. Yet there was never a trace of the sentimental or an acceptance of the cult of the Sublime in his pronouncements. Natural phenomena left him unmoved. He had an ineradicable aversion to children, and he once said to me, "Shall I tell you the most repulsive sentence in creation? 'Have you ever seen a child's hair in the sun?'" His proud motto was, "Es gibt mehr Dinge in unserer Schulweisheit als Erde und Himmel sich träumen lassen." At the end of an electrifying evening with Ernst Kantorowicz in which the topic of discussion had been man's innate sense of the Sublime, EKa, stepping out of the house on Battle Road, remarked, "Looking at the stars, I feel my own futility." To which Panofsky replied, "All I feel is the futility of the stars" (February 18, 1952).

Despite endless and fruitful exchanges of ideas and information which he imparted to and elicited from friends and colleagues, Panofsky kept his work under cover, as it were. Anything worthy of the term "research" was to him a one-man job. Conversely, he remained to the end deeply suspicious of any kind of computerized knowledge, of data retrieval systems, of iconological institutes, and of index work carried out by "little people"; none of these, he was convinced, were capable of making meaningful contributions to the humanities. I once asked him (June 27, 1953) why he had so strenuously (and effectively) resisted the grandiose plan of his friend Fritz Saxl, continued for a while by Saxl's successor at the Warburg Institute, to create an equivalent for the Renaissance of Pauly-Wissowa's *Real-Encyclopädie* of classical antiquity. As so often when he was dead earnest, he smiled. And his tantalizingly satirical answer was, "You mean, all pull together—in the wrong direc-

fig. 4.   Erwin Panofsky at Stanford University, 1964. Princeton, Dr. Gerda Panofsky.

tion?" Everything in humanistic scholarship, even the (to him somewhat comical) New Criticism, which he characterized with Pierrot's words, "Je sais bien écrire, mais je ne sais pas lire," he considered acceptable, so long as it was not "institutionalized." This is why he loved, and rightly so, Guy de Tervarent's one-man job, *Attributs et symboles dans l'art profane,*[14] and why he praised, again rightly so, the superb catalogue of the Early Netherlandish School by Martin Davies of the London National Gallery. He called the latter work "not so much a work of reference but a series of highly concentrated little monographs."

Dora Panofsky died after a long and trying illness. Soon thereafter, Panofsky married Gerda Soergel. Whereas until then he had adjusted his mode of living to that of an invalid, the last two years of his life were truly happy and eventful. For although frail, and now often beset by illness himself, Panofsky enjoyed travel abroad with the youthful enthusiasm that had been dormant for so long. New honors and awards came his way. Some gratified his ego; others, much to his chagrin, were thrust upon him. While he might say with regard to the former, "he got all sorts of medals—he was a real terror," he cited for the latter, not without a certain trace of bitterness, the words of Boethius in prison: "Quis illos igitur putet beatos/ Quos miseri tribuunt honores?" (Who can deem those honors worthwhile that are awarded by the unworthy?).

Old age and death were much-dreaded enemies to Panofsky. Toward the end of his life he circled them restlessly in his own mind. At forty-four "Pan" (as his friends called him) had written an essay on the conception of transcience in Poussin and Watteau, under the title, "Et in Arcadia ego" [Bibl. 63]. Arcadia, according to Virgil an ideal realm of perfect bucolic bliss, was the abode of the pagan god Pan. As Panofsky pointed out, the Renaissance turned the visionary kingdom of Arcadia into a utopian paradise "wrapped in a subtle veil of melancholy" because it was not only the place of love but also of death. As he showed with philological perspicuity, it was Death who in fact must be understood to have uttered the ominous words of the title: "Even in Arcadia, there am I [Death]."[15]

In an almost magical gesture, the aging Panofsky summoned all his mental equipment and called upon his vast store of historical knowledge to reveal in his book on tomb sculpture (1964) the mysteries of man's manipulation of the dead through the ages. He did this with incredible virtuosity in a survey that by far surpassed anything that had ever been written on the theme.

A poem which he composed *sub umbra mortis* will help to hint at that "sweetness and bitterness intermingled" that those last years held for Erwin Panofsky:

Dulcia sane et amara simul praebere senectus
  Cernitur, atque mihi munus utrumque placet.
Pallescunt frondes; stellae tamen usque manebunt.
  Lucet, non urit Sole cadente Venus.

(The impact of sweet as well as bitter events seems, as we must admit, to announce
  the arrival of Old Age.
Both are equally welcome to me in their challenge.

Thus, when leaves turn pale—the stars will remain,
  forever unchanged.
And as the sun sets, Venus lights up, yet no longer burns.)

fig. 5. Erwin Panofsky, 1935. Silverpoint drawing by William Sebastian Heckscher.
Princeton, Dr. Gerda Panofsky.

Dulcia sane et amara simul praebere senectus
Cernitur, atque mihi ——— utrumque placet.
Pallescunt frondes; stellae tamen usque —
Lucet, non urit Sole cadente Venus.

Guilelmo suo in proximum annum
laeta ominatur,
                Pan

The last line of Panofsky's manuscript dedication of the poem to Heckscher reads *Guilelmo suo in proximum annum/ laeta ominatur, Pan* (To his William he wishes happy things in the coming year, Pan). —Ed.

Panofsky Publications Cited by Heckscher

(Numbers correspond to those in the bibliography of
Panofsky's writings cited in n. 3, p. 199 below.)

1. *Die theoretische Kunstlehre Albrecht Dürers (Dürers Ästhetik)*, Berlin, 1914.
2. *Dürers Kunsttheorie, vornehmlich in ihrem Verhältnis zur Kunsttheorie der Italiener*, Berlin, 1915.
14. "Die Entwicklung der Proportionslehre als Abbild der Stilentwicklung," *Monatshefte für Kunstwissenschaft*, 14, 1921, pp. 188–219.
24. *'Idea.' Ein Beitrag zur Begriffsgeschichte der älteren Kunsttheorie*, Leipzig and Berlin, 1924.
36. "Die Perspektive als 'Symbolische Form'," *Vorträge der Bibliothek Warburg*, 1924/25, Leipzig and Berlin, 1927, pp. 258–330.
45. *Herkules am Scheidewege und andere antike Bildstoffe in der neueren Kunst*, Leipzig and Berlin, 1930.
56. "Classical Mythology in Mediaeval Art" (with Fritz Saxl), *Metropolitan Museum Studies*, 1, 1933, pp. 228–80.
63. "Et in Arcadia ego. On the Conception of Transience in Poussin and Watteau," in R. Klibansky and H. J. Paton, eds., *Philosophy and History. Essays Presented to Ernst Cassirer*, Oxford, 1936, pp. 223–54.
64. "On Movies," *Princeton University, Department of Art and Archaeology, Bulletin*, 1936, pp. 5–15.
74. *Studies in Iconology. Humanistic Themes in the Art of the Renaissance*, New York, 1939.
78. "The History of Art as a Humanistic Discipline," in T. M. Greene, ed., *The Meaning of the Humanities*, Princeton, 1940, pp. 89–118.
84. *Albrecht Dürer*, Princeton, 1943.
90. *Abbot Suger on the Abbey Church of St.-Denis and Its Art Treasures*, Princeton, 1946.
106. *Gothic Architecture and Scholasticism*, Latrobe, Pa., 1951.
112. *Early Netherlandish Painting. Its Origins and Character*, Cambridge, Mass., 1953.
115. "The History of Art," in W. R. Crawford, ed., *Cultural Migration*, Philadelphia, 1953, pp. 82–111.
116. "In Defense of the Ivory Tower," *Association of Princeton Graduate Alumni. Report of the Third Conference*, Princeton, 1953, pp. 77–84.
117. *Galileo as a Critic of the Arts*, The Hague, 1954.
120. "Charles Rufus Morey (1877–1955)," *American Philosophical Society Year Book*, 1955, pp. 482–91.
122. *Pandora's Box. The Changing Aspects of a Mythical Symbol* (with Dora Panofsky), New York, 1956.
129. "The Iconography of the Galérie François Ier at Fontainebleau" (with Dora Panofsky), *Gazette des Beaux-Arts*, 52, 1958, pp. 113–90.

132. "Review of Guy de Tervarent, *Attributs et symboles dans l'art profane, 1450–1600, I,*" *Art Bulletin,* 41, 1959, pp. 107–8.

134. *Renaissance and Renascences in Western Art,* Stockholm [1960].

138. "*Canopus Deus,* the Iconography of a Non-existent God," *Gazette des Beaux-Arts,* 57, 1961.

141. "Homage to Fracastoro in a Germano-Flemish Composition of about 1590?," *Nederlands Kunsthistorisch Jaarboek,* 12, 1961, pp. 1–33.

143. *Sokrates in Hamburg,* Hamburg, 1962.

155. "The Ideological Antecedents of the Rolls-Royce Radiator," *Proceedings of the American Philosophical Society,* 107, 1963, pp. 273–88.

160. *Tomb Sculpture. Four Lectures on Its Changing Aspects from Ancient Egypt to Bernini,* New York, 1964.

161. "The Mouse that Michelangelo Failed to Carve," *Marsyas. Studies in the History of Art* (Suplement I, Essays in Memory of Karl Lehmann), New York, 1964.

162. "*Sol Aequinoctialis Fuit Creatus.* Notes on a Composition by Lelio Orsi and Its Possible Connection with the Gregorian Calendar Reform," in *Mélanges Alexandre Koyré,* vol. II, Paris, 1964, pp. 360–80.

Notes

Introduction

1. The first essay is heretofore unpublished, the other two are not currently available (see the publication notes); the fourth, to be mentioned presently, is still in print.

2. It should be emphasized that while he fully appreciated the central importance of connoisseurship, that is, the attribution and dating of works of art on the basis of comparative formal analysis (see his *Meaning in the Visual Arts. Papers in and on Art History*, New York, 1955, 19f.), Panofsky was primarily concerned with the contextual and conceptual aspects of the history of style.

3. On Panofsky's relation to Wölfflin and Riegl generally, see the relevant chapters in M. A. Holly, *Panofsky and the Foundations of Art History* (Ithaca and London, 1984), 36–68, 69–96. For a complete bibliography of Panofsky's writings, see H. Oberer and E. Verheyen, eds., *Erwin Panofsky. Aufsätze zu Grundfragen der Kunstwissenschaft* (Berlin, 1974), 1–17 (copy with addenda by Gerda Panofsky through 1992 in the library of the Institute for Advanced Study, Princeton, NJ). Some studies on Panofsky that have appeared since Holly's book include S. Ferretti, *Cassirer, Panofsky, and Warburg* (New Haven and London, 1984), 142–236; D. Preziosi, *Rethinking Art History. Meditations on a Coy Science* (New Haven and London, 1989), 111–21; J. Lucio de Campos, *Do simbolico ao virtual: a representacao do espaco em Panofsky e Francastel* (São Paulo, 1990); G. Didi-Huberman, *Devant l'image. Question posée aux fins d'une histoire de l'art* (Paris, 1990); N. F. Cantor, *Inventing the Middle Ages. The Lives, Works, and Ideas of the Great Medievalists of the Twentieth Century* (New York, 1991), 174–89; E. Panofsky, *Perspective as Symbolic Form*, trans. C. S. Wood (New York, 1991) (review by J. L. Koerner, "The Shock of the View," *The New Republic*, 26 April 1993, 32–38); J. Hart, "Erwin Panofsky and Karl Mannheim: A Dialogue on Interpretation," *Critical Inquiry* 19 (1993): 534–66; M. Iversen, *Alois Riegl: Art History and Theory* (Cambridge, MA, and London, 1993); C. Cieri Via, *Nei dettagli nascosto. Per una storia del pensiero iconologico,* (Rome, 1994) (with extensive bibliography); C. Landauer, "Erwin Panofsky and the Renascence of the Renaissance," *Renaissance Quarterly* 47 (1994): 255–81; B. Reudenbach, ed., *Erwin Panofsky. Beiträge des Symposions. Hamburg 1992* (Berlin, 1994); I. Lavin, ed., *Meaning in the Visual Arts: Views from the Outside. A Centennial Commemoration of Erwin Panofsky (1892–1968)* (Princeton, forthcoming).

4. After a long absence, style was more or less explicitly the issue in two sessions at the February 1994 meeting of the College Art Association.

5. Panofsky was a vivacious and inspiring speaker, and much in demand. Many of his English-language publications, including virtually all the major ones—*Studies in Iconology* (1939), *Albrecht Dürer* (1943), *Early Netherlandish Painting*

(1953), *Renaissance and Renascences* (1960, a Swedish lecture series), *Tomb Sculpture* (1964), *Problems in Titian* (1969, posthumous)—were first presented as public lectures, often for "mixed audiences"; this congenial format, for which the number and character of American institutions provided a flood of opportunities, complemented the intellectual and professional transformation that Panofsky himself described (see p. 14). Even so, they are also eminently scholarly contributions and sweeping syntheses like those offered here are rare.

6. *Zeitschrift für Ästhetik und allgemeine Kunstwissenschaft* 10 (1915): 460–67.

7. Latrobe, PA, 1951.

8. "The History of the Theory of Human Proportions as a Reflection of the History of Styles" (originally published in German in 1921), in his *Meaning in the Visual Arts* (cited in note 2 herein), 1–25; on perspective, see note 3 herein; on Galileo, see "Galileo as a Critic of the Arts. Aesthetic Attitude and Scientific Thought," *Isis* 47 (1956): 3–15.

9. *Albrecht Dürer* (Princeton, 1943), 63 ff.; *Die deutsche Plastik des elften bis dreizehnten Jahrhunderts* (Munich, 1924); *Early Netherlandish Painting. Its Origins and Character* (Cambridge, MA, 1953).

10. A minor instance, often misinterpreted as signifying a complete lack of sympathy for modern art on Panofsky's part, was a letter to the editor of *Art News*, in which he corrected the caption giving the Latin title of a painting by Barnett Newman (see *Art News* 60, 2 [1961]: 6), and the ensuing exchange (see *Art News* 60, 3 [1961]: 6; *Art News* 60, 5 [1961]: 6). This episode has been mentioned by K. Michels, "Bemerkungen zu Panofskys Sprache," in Reudenbach, cited in note 3 herein *Panofsky. Beiträge des Symposions. Hamburg 1992* (Berlin, 1994), 59–69, cf. p. 63 f., and discussed at length by B. Wyss, "Ein Druckfehler," ibid., 191–99.

11. The lecture was evidently composed between November 7, 1934, and May 3, 1935 (see note 13 herein). The talk may have originated as the introductory lecture, titled "General Characteristics and Foundations of Baroque Art," to a course Panofsky gave at the Institute of Fine Arts on "Principles of Baroque Art" in the spring semester of 1933 (he had come to New York to teach several times before he immigrated; see p. 181), and repeated in the fall of 1936. (I am indebted to Joan Leibovitz of the institute staff for checking Panofsky's course listings on my behalf.) The subjects of the lectures listed for the second course correspond to those summarized in an undated mimeographed pamphlet in the library of the Institute of Fine Arts, New York University: "Italian Baroque Art.

A Syllabus of Lectures given by Prof. Erwin Panofsky. New York University."
There is also a twenty-one-page mimeographed bibliography for the course,
"NYU Fine Arts 265 Bibliography: Principles of Baroque Art by Erwin Panofsky (Revised by Alice Robinson)." This origin may explain the discrepancy between the generic title and the Italian orientation of the text itself.

12. Panofsky's reticence concerning the lecture, especially in later years, is evident
from various references to it in his correspondence. I include here transcriptions
of these passages, my knowledge of which I owe almost entirely to the kindness
of Dieter Wuttke, who is preparing an edition of Panofsky's letters (abbrevia-
tions: WI = Warburg Institute; GC = Getty Center; AAA = Archives of
American Art):

> April 27, 1935, to Fritz Saxl: "Ich habe hier einen sehr generellen Vortrag
> über Barock dreimal in Princeton und zweimal in anderen Orten halten
> müssen." (Here I have given a very general lecture on the Baroque, three
> times in Princeton and twice in other places.)   (WI)

> March 20, 1936, to W. S. Heckscher: "Ein amerikanischer Verleger will
> eventuell eine kleine Sammlung von 'essays' haben (Vorträge im Stil von
> 'What is Baroque?' und ältere Aufsätze ad usum Delphinorum), aber Ich
> glaube, für so etwas bin ich noch nicht alt und bedeutend genug." (An
> American publisher wants possibly to have a small collection of "essays"
> [lectures in the style of "What is Baroque?" and older papers useful for stu-
> dents], but I believe I am not yet old and important enough for such a
> thing.)   (GC)

> June 22, 1946, to Heckscher: "Concerning Baroque as a style, I can only
> refer your friend to a forthcoming article by W. Stechow (Oberlin College,
> Oberlin, Ohio) but I do not know whether he has already proof prints and
> would be willing to give them *avant la lettre*. Another impending article by
> U. Middeldorf (Chicago University) is concerned with the vicissitudes of
> the term and will certainly be of interest but has not appeared either so far
> as I know. In the mean time, I am sending along an unpretentious lecture
> of my own fabrication which you may pass on to Mr. Daniells if *you are sure
> that he will return it*. I may want to use it again if occasion offers. It is not
> very good and full of typographical and other errors but he may get some
> ideas, if only by way of opposition."   (GC)

> February 17, 1947, to Judith B. Williams, Department of History, Wellesley
> College: "As for the topic, I am not quite clear whether you are thinking of
> a general lecture trying to define what baroque art is or of a more specialized
> subject within the baroque period. Supposing the first of these alternatives
> to be true, I suggest the title 'What is Baroque?' This is, of course, a rather
> superficial characterization of the style but might stimulate further reflec-
> tion. In the alternative case, I could only offer a kind of monographic treat-
> ment of the Arkadia theme which is, in my opinion, more rewarding but

has, naturally, not much bearing upon the general question as to how baroque might be defined.   (AAA)

January 22, 1951, to Adolph Katzenellenbogen, Vassar: "If my memory does not fail me, an old lecture of mine entitled, 'What is Baroque?' was once mimeographed by your industrious Vassar girls. I wonder if there are still copies around. If so, would it be possible for me to acquire one or two since I lost my own old typescript?"   (AAA)

February 19, 1960, to William B. Walker, librarian, Brooklyn Museum: "If memory serves that lecture on the Baroque was delivered at Vassar College about thirty years ago, at a time when the word 'Baroque' was still employed as a term of opprobrium in the Anglo-Saxon countries, and would seem to be pretty much out-of-date after a whole generation of art historians, Americans and others, have devoted so much effort to the exploration of Baroque art. I have heard that some industrious Vassar girl typed and mimeographed the lecture at the time but do not own a copy of this document (if it exists) myself. Thus, if you are not deterred by this note, I should advise you to write to the Chairman of the Art Department at Vassar, Mrs. Agnes Claflin."   (AAA)

November 14, 1967, to P. Chobanian, librarian, Ripon College: "I am very flattered by your inquiry about a lecture called 'What is Baroque?' given at Bryn Mawr in 1938. Unfortunately, I am unable to comply with your request for a photoprint of it. The lecture was given thirty years ago, when the term Baroque was not as yet employed in the sense of a definite or at least definable period of art history but merely in a derogatory sense. In the meantime a whole library has been written about Baroque as an art-historical concept so that what made sense and even may have been necessary in 1938 would be entirely superfluous today. For this reason the lecture was never published and I still do not like to have it circulated in writing."   (AAA)

13. Notices concerning the Vassar conference, at which Panofsky gave the lecture on May 3, 1935, are preserved in the Special Collections of Vassar College Library; I am indebted to Stephen Ostrow for unearthing this material on my behalf. The mimeographed version is mentioned by F. Hartt, *Love in Baroque Art* (Locust Valley, NY, 1964), 29 (as having been delivered as a lecture at Bryn Mawr in 1938), and C. H. Smyth, "The Department of Fine Arts for Graduate Students at New York University," in C. H. Smyth and P. M. Lukehart, eds., *The Early Years of Art History in the United States. Notes and Essays on Departments, Teaching, and Scholars* (Princeton, 1993), 73–83, cf. p. 76f.
    There are a total of four versions of the text: (1) a typescript with autograph revisions, one page typed on the back of a letter to Panofsky dated November 7, 1934 (in the possession of Gerda Panofsky); (2) a clean copy of version

1 with autograph revisions (also with Gerda Panofsky); (3) the mimeographed text (a clean copy of version 2; judging from the letters of 1951, 1960, and 1967, cited in the preceding note, Panofsky himself did not have a complete copy of this version—which bears the subtitle "Summary of a lecture by Prof. Erwin Panofsky," although it contains the entire text); (4) a version incorporating most of the mimeographed pages, but with extensive deletions and typed additions (with Gerda Panofsky). The present edition is based on the fourth version (see note on p. 19), which I am unable to date precisely, except that it presumably postdates Panofsky's 1960 reply to the librarian of the Brooklyn Museum in 1960 (see the preceding note). In fact, Panofsky was prepared to include the paper in a series of lectures at the University of California at Santa Barbara in May 1961; learning at the last minute of the loyalty oath required by the University of California, he refused to comply and canceled the engagement. (I owe my awareness of this remarkable episode to Dieter Wuttke, who provided copies of the records in the Archives of American Art; Alexander Sesonske, then professor in the Department of Philosophy, with whom Panofsky corresponded, kindly supplied additional materials from his personal files.)

14. *Kunstgeschichtliche Grundbegriffe. Das Problem der Stilentwicklung in der neueren Kunst* (Munich, 1915) (English edition, London, 1932; reprint, New York, 1950). Wölfflin was by no means unappreciative of the cultural and historical contexts of style, as is evident from the chapter on "The Causes of the Changes in Style" in his earlier work, *Renaissance und Barock* (Basel, 1888) (English edition, Ithaca, 1966); what he sought here was an inner, organic nexus between the specific creative act and such general phenomena. His ultimate purpose was to establish an autonomous structure of stylistic development in a framework of visual perception, or "modes of seeing," which he called a "psychology of form" (see M. Jarzombek, "De-Scribing the Language of Looking: Wölfflin and the History of Aesthetic Experientialism," *Assemblage* 23 [1994]: 29–69).

15. See the letters of 1960 and 1967 cited in note 12 herein.

16. See p. 6 and note 2, p. 207.

17. He referred to the lecture variously as "sehr generell" (1935), "unpretentious" and "not very good and full of typographical and other errors" (1946), "a rather superficial characterization of the style" (1947), "out-of-date" (1960), "superfluous today" (1967); see note 12 herein. Panofsky was given to such self-deprecating remarks, but in this case I think they signify more than simple modesty.

18. See p. 45 and pp. 84–88 below.

19. The very last phrase of the text, "provided that it [our epoch] does not put an end to all generations to come," was added in the fourth version (cf. note 13 herein). For Panofsky's views on the relationship between the active and contemplative life, see his "In Defense of the Ivory Tower," *The Centennial Review of Arts & Science* 1 (1957): 111–22, and the observations in my "Panofsky's History of Art," to be published in I. Lavin, ed., *Meaning in the Visual Arts* (cited in note 3 herein).

20. W. Weibel, *Jesuitismus und Barockskulptur* (Strasbourg, 1909); W. Weisbach, *Der Barock als Kunst der Gegenreformation* (Berlin, 1921; H. Tintelnot, *Barocktheater und barocke Kunst. Die Entwicklungsgeschichte der Fest-und Theater-dekoration in ihrem Verhältnis zur barocken Kunst* (Berlin, 1929). Other interpretations of the Baroque include relating the style to the emergence of the modern state (C. J. Friedrich, *The Age of the Baroque 1610–1660* [New York, 1952]) and the classical tradition of rhetoric (see *Rettorica e barocco. Atti del III congresso internazionale di studi umanistici* [Rome, 1955]).
    For a helpful survey of literature on the Baroque generally, see D. A. Carozza, *European Baroque. A Selective Bibliography* (Norwood, PA, 1977).

21. H. Bredekamp has observed (see "*Ex Nihilo:* Panofsky's Habilitation," in Reudenbach, cited in note 3 herein, pp. 31–51, cf. p. 44) that Panofsky specifically lamented Wölfflin's progressive tendency to exclude psychological factors in art ("Heinrich Wölfflin [Zu seinem 60. Geburtstage am 21. Juni 1924]," reprinted in Oberer and Verheyen, cited in note 3 herein, pp. 45–48, cf. p. 46). Panofsky's notion of psychology in this context involved consciousness, emotional states, and so forth, as distinct from Wölfflin's concern with perception (note 13 herein).

22. See "On Movies," *Bulletin of the Department of Art and Archaeology of Princeton University* (June 1936): 5–15 (the date is mistakenly given as 1934 in some sources); "Style and Medium in the Moving Pictures," *Transition* 26 (1937): 121–33, and "Style and Medium in the Moving Pictures," in D. L. Durling, *A Preface to Our Day* (New York, 1940), 57–82; "Style and Medium in the Motion Pictures," *Critique. A Review of Contemporary Art* 1 (1947): 5–28 (the evaluation I quote is from the editors' preliminary note).

23. Perhaps the nearest analogy is the twelfth-century Abbot Suger's commentary on the new Gothic architecture at St.-Denis, a text Panofsky had published in his celebrated edition, *Abbot Suger on the Abbey Church of St.-Denis and Its Art Treasures* (Princeton, 1946), the year before he revised the movie essay. The connection is not as farfetched as it may seem and, curiously enough, the link may

have been the *New Yorker* magazine. In his memorial, reprinted in this volume, William Heckscher has pointed to the stylish *New Yorker* profile genre as an inspiration for Panofsky's biographical essay on Suger (see p. 184 below), and Panofsky himself makes reference to the *New Yorker* in his study of the film (see p. 102 below).

24. As noted by D. Talbot, ed., *Film. An Anthology* (New York, 1959), 15. Margaret Scolari Barr, wife of Alfred H. Barr, Director of the Museum of Modern Art, was a student in Panofsky's first seminar in America (see the eulogy by Millard Meiss in *A Commemorative Gathering for Erwin Panofsky at the Institute of Fine Arts New York University in Association with the Institute for Advanced Study* [New York, 1968], 9), and they remained lifelong friends. Heckscher (see p. 000 below) provides some personal reminiscences of Panofsky on the movies, including his delight during 1946–47 in giving the talk (evidently the newly revised version), followed by a showing of a silent film such as Buster Keaton's *The Navigator* with comic commentary.

25. Panofsky recounted the facts and repercussions of his move to America in "Three Decades of Art History in the United States. Impressions of a Transplanted European," in his *Meaning in the Visual Arts* (cited in note 2 herein), 321–46, cf. p. 321 f.; see also Heckscher (see pp. 000–000 below); and now C. H. Smyth, as in note 13 herein.

26. Panofsky expresses his appreciation of this peculiarly American urbanity in his autobiographical essay, cited in the preceding note. On the importance for Panofsky of the intellectual environment of Princeton at that time—especially the emphasis on a broad, interdisciplinary approach to cultural history, which he must have found very congenial—see the contribution of C. H. Smyth, "Thoughts on Erwin Panofsky's First Years in Princeton," in Lavin, ed., *Meaning in the Visual Arts* (cited in note 3 herein).

27. The popular German coinage "Kino" refers to the theater, not the film itself; the equally colloquial English "flick" refers to the effect of light, rather than of movement, which was Panofsky's primary concern.

28. The tradition is far from obsolete. Albeit in different contexts and guises, the effort to characterize ethnically and geographically defined styles might be said to underlie recent works such as M. Baxandall, *Painting and Experience in Fifteenth Century Italy. A Primer in the Social History of Pictorial Style* (Oxford, 1972), and S. Alpers, *The Art of Describing. Dutch Art in the Seventeenth Century* (Chicago, 1983); and it continues to pervade the current preoccupation with multiculturalism.

29. On this last point, it is curious to note that Pevsner (p. 9) praises Frey's book as being "absolutely free" from any "Nazi bias," whereas by the time the work was published Frey had participated in the plundering of the Royal Castle at Warsaw. See J. Lileyko, *A Companion Guide to the Royal Castle in Warsaw* (Warsaw, 1980), 84; further, H. Dilly, *Deutsche Kunsthistoriker 1933–1945* (Munich and Berlin, 1988), 73; L. H. Nicholas, *The Rape of Europa. The Fate of Europe's Treasures in the Third Reich and the Second World* (New York, 1994), 74f., reports that Frey opposed the destruction of the castle.

30. Philadelphia, November 8, 1962.

31. In his canonical introduction to *Studies in Iconology* (New York and Evanston, 1962), 3–31, Panofsky places style at the *primary* or *natural* level of the interpretation of the work of art, in that style (expressive form) is the means through which we recognize the meaning of motifs. On the relation of style to "iconography" and "contextualism" in Panofsky's art history, see Holly, as in note 2 herein, passim; also my "Iconography as a Humanistic Discipline. ('Iconography at the Crossroads')," in B. Cassidy, *Iconography at the Crossroads* (Princeton, 1992), 33–42, and "Panofsky's History of Art" (cited in note 19 herein).

32. *Renaissance and Renascences in Western Art* (Stockholm, 1960).

33. It is certainly "amusing" in the Panofskyan sense that the one explicitly humorous work he wrote in German is one of his few publications (all memoirs of former friends and colleagues) in his native language after he emigrated, in a Festschrift devoted to his beloved teacher Adolph Goldschmidt, entitled "Goldschmidts Humor" (*Adolph Goldschmidt zum Gedächtnis. 1863–1944*) (Hamburg, 1963), 25–32. The early essay "Sokrates in Hamburg oder Vom Schönen und Guten" hardly counts in this respect since it was published under the pseudonym A. F. Synkop, in a literary rather than a scholarly journal (*Querschnitt* 11 [1931]: 593–99; reprinted in *Idea. Jahrbuch der Hamburger Kunsthalle* 1 [1982]: 9–15).

34. See his "Three Decades," cited in note 25 herein. The transformation of Panofsky's language has been perceptively discussed by Michels, cited in note 10 herein.

35. Hugo Buchthal, recalling Panofsky as a teacher in Hamburg, stressed his warmth, generosity, and keen sense of humor in the commemoration cited in note 24 herein, 11–14; the epitaph was reported by Harry Bober in the same publication (see p. 20). Panofsky's personal qualities, as well as his intellectual

gifts, are evoked in every memorial of him (for a list see H. van de Waal, "In Memoriam. Erwin Panofsky. March 30, 1892–March 14, 1968," *Mededelingen der koninklijke nederlands Akademie van Wetenschappen, Afd. Letterkunde* 35 [1972]: 227–44, cf. pp. 242–44).

What Is Baroque?

1. The first four paragraphs were added in the fourth version of the paper (see note 12 above). Here Panofsky's typescript contains a footnote reference to a review by A. Castro of L. Pfandi, *Historia de la literatura nacional española*, in *Revista de filología española* 21 (1934): 66–77, in which this etymology is briefly discussed on p. 76. Much more detailed studies of the various theories of the derivation of the term will be found in O. Kurz, "Barocco: storia di una parola," *Lettere italiane* 12 (1960): 414–44, and B. Migliorini, "Etimologia e storia del termine 'barocco,'" in *Manierismo, barocco, rococò: concetti e termini. Convegno internazionale, Roma 21–24 Aprile 1960* (Rome, 1962), 39–54 (Accademia nazionale dei lincei. Anno CCCLIX, 1962. Relazioni e discussioni).

2. Panofsky reiterates a standard critique of Wölfflin, who failed to recognize the nature and autonomy of the development that intervened between the Renaissance and the Baroque, now commonly defined in three phases: mannerism, Maniera, and the antimannerist reaction around 1600. This basic structure had been laid out by Panofsky's close friend, Walter Friedlaender, in two pioneering studies of 1925 and 1930, published in English as *Mannerism and Anti-Mannerism in Italian Painting* (New York, 1957), with a helpful introduction by D. Posner; see further the classic essay by C. H. Smyth, *Mannerism and Maniera* (Vienna, 1992). Panofsky's contribution was to see the whole development consistently in relation to deep changes in the cultural "psyche," as distinct from Wölfflin's psychology of perception.

3. The idea of merging the arts was first defined and effected by Bernini; see I. Lavin, *Bernini and the Unity of the Visual Arts* (New York and Oxford, 1980).

4. The "frontality" of Baroque sculpture was observed by R. Wittkower, in "Le Bernin et le baroque romain," *Gazette des beaux-arts* 11 (1934): 327–41.

5. Panofsky refers to the vogue for the austere, black, Spanish fashion in clothes, and to Tasso's voluntary submission of the text of his *Gerusalemme Liberata* to the censors of the Inquisition.

6. Panofsky here refers to the loincloths painted over Michelangelo's nude figures later in the sixteenth century.

7. To my knowledge, the pioneer observer of the reprise of mannerism in the late Baroque and Rococo was N. Pevsner. See N. Pevsner (with O. Grautoff), *Barockmalerei in den romanischen Länder* (Wildpark-Potsdam, 1928), 193 ff.

8. Panofsky here refers to the dramatic stories told by Bernini's biographers concerning the flaws that appeared in the marble for the bust and the artist's fall from favor under Innocent X—both potential catastrophes that were averted by Bernini's extraordinary wit and virtuosity. See F. Baldinucci, *Vita del cavaliere Gio. Lorenzo Bernino* (Florence, 1682), ed. S. S. Ludovici, Milan, 1948, 76 f., 101 ff. (trans. by C. Enggass, *The Life of Bernini*, University Park, PA, and London, 1966, 11 f., 35 ff.); D. Bernini, *Vita del cavalier Gio. Lorenzo Bernino* (Rome: 1713), 10 f., 84 ff.

9. In a letter of May 5, 1631, from Amsterdam, to the writer Jean-Louis Guez de Balzac (1595–1654), who had mentioned his intention to withdraw from the life at court, Descartes offers amusingly ironic praise for Amsterdam, which he prefers

> not only to all the convents of the Capuchins or Carthusians, where fine people retire, but also to the most beautiful dwellings of France and Italy. . . . However commodious a country house might be, it always lacks an infinity of conveniences that are only to be found in cities; and even the solitude one hopes for is never really perfect. I admit you may find a canal that would make the most garrulous dream, and a valley so solitary as to inspire them with transport and joy; but it would be hard to avoid a quantity of little neighbors who will sometimes annoy you, and whose visits are even more disturbing than those you receive in Paris. By contrast, in the great city where I am, there being no one, except me, who is not a merchant, everyone is so attentive to his profit that I could live here my whole life without ever being seen by anyone. I stroll every day among the confusion of great crowds with as much liberty and repose as you can find in your paths, and I do not view the people I see other than I do the trees one encounters in your forests or the animals that pass there. Even the noise of their bustle no more interrupts my reveries than would that of some stream. If I sometimes reflect on their activities, I do so with the same pleasure you have in watching the peasants cultivate the countryside, for I see that all their labor serves to embellish the place where I live and assure that I want for nothing. For if there is pleasure in watching the fruits grow in your orchards and fill the eyes with abundance, there is no less in seeing arrive here the ships that bring us in abundance all that the Indies produce, and all that is rare in Europe. What other place in the world could one choose where all the conveniences of life and every curiosity one could wish were as easy to find as here? In what other country could one enjoy such complete liberty, or sleep with less anxiety, where there are always soldiers under foot to guard us, where poisonings, betrayals and calumnies are less rare and where there remains more of the innocence of our ancestors? I do not see how you can so love the air of Italy, with which one so often inhales the plague, and where the heat of the day is always intolerable and the coolness of eve-

ning unhealthy, and where the obscurity of night covers larcenies and murders. If you fear the winters of the north, tell me what shadows, what fan, what fountains can so well protect you from the annoyance of the heat at Rome, as a stove and a big fire will exempt you here from the cold.

My translation; see A. Bridoux, *Descartes. Oeuvres et lettres* (Paris, 1949), 728–30.

10. This remarkable painting, formerly in private hands and now lost, was published by W. von Bode, "Kunsthistorische Ausbeute aus dem Deutschen Kunsthandel von Heute. 4. Adriaen Brouwer," *Repertorium für Kunstwissenschaft* 49 (1928): 8–11, and R. Hamman, "Kunst als Protest (Zur niederländischen Malerei des 17. Jahrhunderts)," in *Richard Hamann in Memoriam* (Berlin, 1963), 79–100, cf. 99f.

11. Panofsky's discussion of caricature was evidently indebted to that of Wittkower (in H. Brauer and R. Wittkower, *Die Zeichnungen des Gianlorenzo Bernini* [Berlin, 1931], 180–84), who also regarded caricature as the earmark of a new, modern world view; Panofsky extended the idea to incorporate the distinction between satire and humor, and a psychology of self-awareness. When Panofsky wrote, the study of caricature was much in vogue. In 1934 a major historical work appeared that included caricature by W. R. Juynboll (*Het komische genre in de italiaansche Schilderkonst gedurende de 17 en 18 eeuw*, Leiden), and a psychoanalytical approach was taken by E. Kris in an article in Freud's journal. See E. Kris, "Zur Psychologie der Karikatur," *Imago. Zeitschrift für psychoanalytische Psychologie, ihre Grenzgebiete und Anwendung* 20: 450–66. Kris there announces a joint historical study in preparation with Ernst Gombrich, which appeared as "The Principles of Caricature," *British Journal of Medical Psychology* 17 (1938): 319–42 (both papers reprinted in E. Kris, *Psychoanalytic Explorations in Art* [New York, 1952], 173–203), and resulted in their small volume *Caricature* (London, 1940).

　　　The episode in Paris is described in P. Fréart de Chantelou's famous diary of Bernini's visit in 1665 (*Journal du voyage du Cavalier Bernin en France*, ed. L. Lalanne [Paris, 1885], 106; *Diary of the Cavaliere Bernini's Visit to France*, ed. A. Blunt, trans. by M. Corbet, annotated by G. C. Bauer [Princeton, 1985], 129f.). On Bernini and caricature, see I. Lavin, "High and Low before Their Time: Bernini and the Art of Social Satire," in K. Varnedoe and A. Gopnik, eds., *Modern Art and Popular Culture. Readings in High and Low* (New York, 1990), 18–50.

12. C. R. Morey, *Mediaeval Art* (New York, 1942), 4: "[Christianity] as the determinant of thought and expression . . . began to disappear with the rise of the Renaissance in the fifteenth century, when, so to speak, men began to look upon themselves and their surroundings as more interesting than God."

Style and Medium in the Motion Pictures

1. I make this distinction because it was, in my opinion, a fall from grace when *Snow White* introduced the human figure and when *Fantasia* attempted to picturalize The World's Great Music. The very virtue of the animated cartoon is to animate, that is to say endow lifeless things with life, or living things with a different kind of life. It effects a metamorphosis, and such a metamorphosis is wonderfully present in Disney's animals, plants, thunderclouds, and railroad trains. Whereas his dwarfs, glamorized princesses, hillbillies, baseball players, rouged centaurs, and *amigos* from South America are not transformations but caricatures at best, and fakes or vulgarities at worst. Concerning music, however, it should be borne in mind that its cinematic use is no less predicated upon the principle of coexpressibility than is the cinematic use of the spoken word. There is music permitting or even requiring the accompaniment of visible action (such as dances, ballet music, and any kind of operatic compositions) and music of which the opposite is true; and this is, again, not a question of quality (most of us rightly prefer a waltz by Johann Strauss to a symphony by Sibelius) but one of intention. In *Fantasia* the hippopotamus ballet was wonderful, and the Pastoral Symphony and "Ave Maria" sequences were deplorable, not because the cartooning in the first case was infinitely better than in the two others (cf. above), and certainly not because Beethoven and Schubert are too sacred for picturalization, but simply because Ponchielli's "Dance of the Hours" (fig. 13) is coexpressible while the Pastoral Symphony (fig. 14) and the "Ave Maria" are not. In cases like these even the best imaginable music and the best imaginable cartoon will impair rather than enhance each other's effectiveness.

   Experimental proof of all this was furnished by Disney's recent *Make Mine Music* where The World's Great Music was fortunately restricted to Prokofieff. Even among the other sequences the most successful ones were those in which the human element was either absent or reduced to a minimum; Willie the Whale, the Ballad of Johnny Fedora, and Alice Blue-Bonnet, and, above all, the truly magnificent Goodman Quartet.

2. I cannot help feeling that the final sequence of the new Marx Brothers film *Night in Casablanca* (fig. 15)—where Harpo unaccountably usurps the pilot's seat of a big airplane, causes incalculable havoc by flicking one tiny little control after another, and waxes the more insane with joy the greater the disproportion between the smallness of his effort and the magnitude of the disaster—is a magnificent and terrifying symbol of man's behavior in the atomic age. No doubt the Marx Brothers would vigorously reject this interpretation; but so would Dürer have done had anyone told him that his "Apocalypse" foreshadowed the cataclysm of the Reformation.

The Ideological Antecedents of the Rolls-Royce Radiator

1. See M. L. Gothein, *Geschichte der Gartenkunst* (Jena, 1926) 2: p. 367 ff. (English translation: *A History of Garden Art* (London and Toronto, n.d.) 2: p. 279 ff.). Cf. F. Kimball, "Romantic Classicism in Architecture," *Gazette des Beaux-Arts,* 6th ser., 25 (1944): 95 ff.

2. *Discourses on Art* (New York, Paperback Edition, 1961) 13: p. 210 f.

3. *Moral Essays* 4, "On Taste."

4. *Moral Essays* 4, "On Taste."

5. See E. Gradmann, "Das englische Aquarell," *Festschrift Hans R. Hahnloser* (Basel and Stuttgart, 1961), p. 413 ff., particularly p. 416.

6. *Moral Essays* 4, "On Taste."

7. According to the *Encyclopedia Britannica* the term "Palladianism" is "specifically applied to the architecture of the period 1715–1760 in England, when British taste relied heavily on the designs of Inigo Jones who had introduced High Renaissance architecture into England." For the all-important role of Lord Burlington, which had tended to be severely underestimated, see F. Kimball, "Burlington Architectus," *Jour. Royal Inst. British Architects* 34 (1927): 675 ff., and 35 (1928): 14 ff.; and most particularly, R. Wittkower, *The Earl of Burlington and William Kent* (York Georgian Society, Original Papers, Number Five, 1948), followed by an article in *Bolletino del Centro Internazionale di Storia d'Architetura Andrea Palladio,* no. 2 (Vicenza, 1960).

8. See Pope's amusing poem entitled "The Beaufort House Gateway at Chiswick":
   I was brought from Chelsea last year
   Batter'd with wind and weather;
   Inigo Jones put me together;
   Sir Hans Sloane
   Let me alone;
   Burlington brought me hither.

9. Sir John Clerk, the author of *The Country Seat* (1727), called Chiswick "properly a villa and by much the best in England"; see J. Fleming, *Robert Adam and His Circle in Edinburgh and Rome* (London, 1962; also Cambridge, Mass., 1962), p. 32.

10. See, for example, the Temple of Concord and Victory at Stowe, illustrated in Kimball, "Romantic Classicism in Architecture," fig. 8.

11. See F. Kimball, "Les Influences anglaises dans la formation du style Louis XVI," *Gazette des Beaux-Arts,* 6th ser. 5 (1931): 29ff., 231ff. For English influence on Continental painting, cf. J. Loquin, *La Peinture d'histoire en France de 1747 à 1785 . . .* (Paris, 1912); E. K. Waterhouse, "The British Contribution to the Neo-Classical Style in Painting," *Proc. British Academy* 40 (1955): 57ff.

12. Fleming, op. cit., pl. 37.

13. Fleming, ibid., pl. 86.

14. Fleming, ibid. pls. 23, 24, 25 (all between 1749 and 1753); pl. 87 (1759). It should be noted that at this time the Gothic style was not as yet accepted for serious domestic architecture; a Gothic manor such as Inveraray Castle (Fleming, pl. 20), designed about 1745 by Robert Adam's father, William (who otherwise worked "in the true Palladian taste"), is rather exceptional at that time.

15. Fleming, ibid., pl. 80, and p. 259, fig. 14.

16. Fleming, ibid., p. 243, fig. 12.

17. See S. H. Monk, *The Sublime; A Study of Critical Theories in XVIII-Century England* (Ann Arbor, Mich., Paperback Edition, 1960), pp. 191–202.

18. Monk, ibid., 173: "Michelangelo comes steadily into greater favor after 1750." The climax of his glorification was reached in Fuseli and Reynolds; see, e.g., Reynolds' *Fifth Discourse* (December 19, 1772), ed. cit., p. 76f.: "Michael Angelo has more of the Poetical Inspiration; his ideas are vast and sublime. . . . To the question therefore, which ought to hold the first rank, Raffaelle or Michael Angelo, it must be answered that if it is to be given to him who possessed a greater combination of the higher qualities of the art than any other man, there is no doubt but Raffaelle is the first. But if, as Longinus thinks, the sublime, being the highest excellence that human composition can attain to, abundantly compensates the absence of every other beauty, and atones for all other deficiencies, then Michael Angelo demands the preference." The *Fifteenth Discourse* of December 10, 1790, is almost entirely devoted to the praise of Michelangelo and constant reference is made to his "sublimity," his "most sublime and poetical imagination," etc. (ed. cit., pp. 238, 240). An interesting and relatively early application of the term "sublime" to architecture is found in James Adam's unfinished essay on architecture composed in November 1763 (Fleming, op. cit., p. 317): "[domes] are of themselves one of the most beautiful and most sublime inventions of this or any other art."

19. See L. M. C. Randall, "*Exempla* as a source of Gothic marginal illumination," *Art Bulletin* 39 (1957): 97 ff., with excellent bibliography.

20. E. Millar, *The Rutland Psalter* (Oxford, 1937), fol. 112 v. The drolleries here shown are on fols. 104 and 107 v.

21. See G. M. Trevelyan, *History of England* (New York, Paperback Edition, 1953) 1: p. 309 ff.

22. M. M. Tamir, "The English Origin of the Flamboyant Style," *Gazette des Beaux-Arts*, 6th ser., 29 (1946): 257 ff.; J. Bony, *French Cathedrals* (London, 1951), p. 15. Bony correctly emphasizes that the sources of the Flamboyant Style are not *exclusively* English, that "symptoms" of it appear in French court art even before 1300, and that it may have drawn upon the vocabulary of "miniatures, ivories and tombs" rather than architecture. But he no less correctly adds that such Continental experiments were "short-lived, neither flourishing nor developing to any extent"; and it seems probable that the very "miniatures and ivories" he has in mind (such, for example, as the Belleville Breviary by Jean Pucelle and his collaborators) are not quite independent of insular influence.

23. For the custom of calling the circular windows of the south and north transepts of Lincoln Cathedral, respectively, the "Bishop's Eye" and the "Dean's Eye" (a custom documented from as early as 1220–1235), see the versified *Life of St. Hugh of Lincoln;* reprinted in O. Lehmann-Brockhaus, *Lateinische Schriftquellen zur Kunst in England, Wales und Schottland vom Jahre 901 bis zum Jahre 1307* (Munich, 1955–1960) 2: p. 27 ff., no. 2372.

24. F. Bond, *Gothic Architecture in England* (London, 1906), p. 494.

25. These expressions are borrowed from Giraldus Cambrensis's remarkable description of an Irish manuscript, for which see below, p. 285.

26. Bond, op. cit., p. 494 ff.; G. G. Coulton, *Art and the Reformation* (New York, 1928), p. 19 ff. Cf. J. H. Harvey, "St. Stephen's Chapel and the Origin of the Perpendicular Style," *Burlington Magazine* 88 (1946): 192 ff.

27. For its development from the "lierne" vault, see particularly F. Bond, *An Introduction to English Church Architecture* (London, 1913) 1: p. 339 ff.

28. For a brief and lucid discussion of the genetic problems posed by early insular art see C. Nordenfalk's contribution to A. Grabar and S. Nordenfalk, *Early*

Medieval Painting from the Fourth to the Eleventh Century (Skira Book, 1957), pp. 109–25, particularly p. 118 ff.

29. Trevelyan, op. cit. 1: p. 68.

30. Trevelyan, ibid., p. 30.

31. See note 33.

32. This is in contrast to Continental descriptions of ruins, both earlier and later (Venantius Fortunatus on the one hand, Hildebert of Lavardin, on the other), where the emphasis is first, on the original beauty of the monuments now destroyed ("Roma quanta fuit, ipsa ruina docet"); second, on the hope for a better future. Only the English could, in the eighteenth century, conceive the idea of building *artificial ruins*.

33. I do not believe that direct classical influence can be recognized in a statue at Winchester which H. Roosen-Runge ("Ein Werk englischer Grossplastik und die Antike," *Festschrift Hans R. Hahnloser* (Basel and Stuttgart, 1961), p. 103 ff.) believes to derive from a classical model. In my opinion the work is an offshoot of the north transept sculpture at Chartres.

34. Osbert's statement is quoted in Abbot Samson's *Miracula S. Eadmundi;* see Lehmann-Brockhaus, op. cit. 3: p. 422, no. 6696.

35. John of Salisbury, *Historia pontificalis;* see Lehmann-Brockhaus, op. cit. 2: p. 667, no. 4760 (also quoted by Roosen-Runge, op. cit., and elsewhere); cf. E. Panofsky, *Renaissance and Renascences* (Stockholm, 1960), p. 72 f.

36. Cf. the literature referred to by Panofsky, ibid., p. 73, n. 1.

37. See E. K. Rand, "The Irish Flavor of *Hisperica Famina,*" *Studien zur lateinischen Dichtung des Mittel-alters; Ehrengabe für Karl Strecker zum 4. September 1931* (Dresden, 1931), p. 134 ff. The standard edition of the *Hisperica Famina* is by F. J. H. Jenkinson, *The Hisperica Famina . . .* (Cambridge, 1908), proving (p. x) that "even if the text is not by an Irishman the scene is laid in a country where the language of the inhabitants is Irish" and adding such related texts as the *Lorica,* the *Rubisca,* and the hymn *Adelphus Adelpha.* The *Description of Ireland,* as printed in Bruno Krusch's edition of the *Life of St. Columbanus,* is reprinted and translated in Rand (whose translation is here adopted with only minor modifications); the pertinent passage reads as follows:

> Expectatque Titanis occasum, dum vertitur orbis,
> Lux et occiduas pontum descendit in umbras:

Undarum inmanes moles quo truces latebras
Colore et nimio passim crine crispanti,
Peplo kana, raptim quem dant cerula terga,
Aequoris spumea cedunt et litora, sinus
Ultimus terrarum, nec mitem sinunt carinam
Tremulo petentem salo dare nota litora nobis.
Flavus super haec Titan descendit opago
Lumine Arcturi petitque partes girando:
Aquilonem sequens, orientis petit ad ortum,
Ut mundo redivivus lumen reddat amoenum,
Sese mundo late tremulo ostendat et igne.
Sicque metas omnes diei noctisque peractu
Cursu et inpletas, suo lustrat candore terras,
Amoenum reddens orbem calore madentem.

38. John Dennis, *Miscellanies in Verse and Prose* (London, 1963), p. 133f. (quoted in Monk, op. cit., 207).

39. F. J. E. Raby, *A History of Secular Latin Poetry in the Middle Ages* (Oxford, 1934) 1: p. 175f.

40. St. Columba, quoted in Raby, ibid., p. 164. A similar passage from Alcuin is quoted in Raby, p. 183. St. Columba even knows that the *versus bipedalis* (Adonid) was invented by Sappho.

41. Aldhelm, *De Virginitate,* 45 ff., quoted in Raby, p. 175, n.

42. Raby, 1: p. 155: "It is hard to believe that he had any serious knowledge of quantitative verse." Virgil's discussion of prosody is found in his *Epitome* 4 (E. Huemer, *Virgilii Grammatici Maronis opera* (Leipzig, 1886), p. 12ff.); his level of erudition is characterized by the fact that he defines geometry as "ars disciplinata, quae omnium herbarum graminumque experimentum enunciat."

43. A modern edition of Bede's work is found in E. Keil, *Grammatici latini* (Leipzig, 1880) 7: p. 217ff. It should be noted that Bede takes most of his examples from Christian authors—except for such very famous poets as Virgil, Lucan, and, oddly enough, Lucretius.

44. O. Lehmann-Brockhaus, as quoted in N. Pevsner, *The Englishness of English Art* (London, 1956), p. 27.

45. Burchardus de Hallis, *Chronicon ecclesiae collegiatae S. Petri Winpiensis.* The passage, probably written about 1280 (the author died in 1300), has often been reprinted and discussed, most recently by P. Frankl, *The Gothic; Literary Sources*

and *Interpretations through Eight Centuries* (Princeton, 1960), p. 55f. The phrase *fenestrae et columnae ad instar operis anglici* probably refers to the fact that each of the circular piers has eight disengaged and differentiated colonnettes; the tracery of the windows is unfortunately modern.

46. *Chronica Gervasii Monachi Cantuariensis (ad annum 1174)*; frequently reprinted and translated; the passage here cited is found in Lehmann-Brockhaus, op. cit. 1: p. 230, no. 822.

47. Giraldus Cambrensis, *Topographia Hibernaie*, dist. 2, cap. 38f. (Kildare); reprinted in Lehmann-Brockhaus, op. cit. 3: p. 217, no. 5940.

48. Goscelinus, *Legend of St. Edith in Verse;* reprinted in Lehmann-Brockhaus, op. cit. 2: p. 625 ff., no. 4616.

49. *Chronica de Mailros (ad annum 1216);* reprinted in Lehmann-Brockhaus, op. cit. 3: 127, no. 5573.

50. *Versified Life of St. Hugh of Lincoln* (composed between 1220 and 1235); reprinted in Lehmann-Brockhaus 2: p. 27 ff., no. 2372:
    > Viscosusque liquor lapides conglutinat albos,
    > Quos manus artificis omnes excidit ad unguem.
    > Et paries ex congerie constructus eorum,
    > Hoc quasi dedignans, mentitur continuare
    > Contiguas partes; non esse videtur ab arte,
    > Quin a natura; non res unita, sed una. . . .
    > Inde columnellae, quae sic cinxere columnas,
    > Ut videantur ibi quamdam celebrare choream.

51. Source referred to in note 48. The lines in question read as follows:
    > Vultus intrantum ferit aurea lux populorum
    >   Clarifice
    > Atque repercusso congaudent omnia Phebo
    >   A radiis.

52. Source referred to in note 50.

53. *Wolstani Vita S. Aethelwoldi Episcopi Wintoniensis;* reprinted in Lehmann-Brockhaus, op. cit. 2: p. 650f., no. 4691. The passage in question reads as follows:
    > Stat super auratis virgae fabricatio bullis;
    >   Aureus et totum splendor adornat opus.
    > Luna coronato quoties radiaverit ortu,
    >   Alterum ab aede sacra surgit ad astra iubar:
    > Si nocte inspiciat hunc praetereundo viator,
    >   Et terram stellas credit habere suas.

---

54. Lehmann-Brockhaus, op. cit. 1: p. 217f., no. 800.

55. H. Nockholds, *The Magic of a Name* (revised edition, London, 1950), pp. 42, 251. I owe my acquaintance with this book to Mr. Winthrop Brubaker, Vice-President of Rolls-Royce, Inc., to whom I am also indebted for the photographs reproduced in figs. 19 and 20.

Erwin Panofsky: A Curriculum Vitae

1. There existed plans to resume the *Colloquium* on the Ghent Altarpiece in the summer of 1955. These plans were shelved and ultimately cancelled as a result of the upheavals caused by the van Beuningen affair (letter of May 20, 1955). None of the participants has been able to tell whether there exists or existed a manuscript for the planned publication of what Panofsky referred to as the "Addenda et Corrigenda re Mouton." He spoke, however, in a letter addressed to Emanuel Winternitz (February 16, 1966) of the "somewhat augmented *procès-verbaux*" in his possession but, in the same letter, he made it clear that "after the untimely death of Paul Coremans, there is very little chance that the observations which he, Martin Davies and I made many years ago, first and foremost the essential change of the organ and the hand of the player in the Ghent Altarpiece, will ever be published . . ." It is for these reasons that I feel that I should place on record my notes of the account of the fruitful summer of 1954 that Panofsky gave to me later that year: "The *moutonnements* were real revelations. I had never been inside a picture, so to speak, as you really are when living for weeks in a room the walls of which consist of X-rays illumined from behind. Though I have to give up some of my cherished theories *en détail,* the *whole* of my hypothesis seems to stand up surprisingly well and was even confirmed by some quite new observations. Especially: a basic change of perspective in the altar, the organ and the lectern of the Glee Club which, in *all* these cases, amounts to a fundamental modernization. Originally all these items were rendered in a perspective as archaic as that of the fountain still is—which could not be modernized without destroying the whole composition. Also, the organ was modernized even from a purely technical point of view. Originally there were no black keys of which the present state seems to be the earliest instance. I can almost hear Gilles Binchois coming into Jan's studio, and saying: 'Ah, non, mon vieux, cette orgue de feu ton frère est tout-à-fait démodée; et d'ailleurs, ce n'est pas comme ça qu'on joue.' Originally the keys were not actually depressed, and the hands of the lady-organist were not really bent to playing position, and one hand had no thumb!" Cf. Paul Coremans, "Un colloque international sur 'L'Agneau Mystique,'" *Bulletin Musées Royaux des B.-A.,* 1–3, Brussels, 1955, p. 171f.; E. Panofsky, "Homage à Paul Coremans: The Promoter of a New Co-

operation between the Natural Sciences and the History of Art," *Bulletin de l'Institut Royal du Patrimoine artistique,* 8, 1965, pp. 62–67. Dr. Winternitz was kind enough to make available to me in manuscript a chronological listing of "Keyboard Instruments with white naturals/black sharps"; this only supports Panofsky's suggestion that the black keys in the Ghent Altarpiece constitute a *primordium.*

2. The obiter dicta cited, wherever ascertainable, by date are placed between quotation marks.

3. Panofsky, "Dürer as a Mathematician," *The World of Mathematics. A small library of the literature of mathematics from A'h-mose the Scribe to Albert Einstein, presented with commentaries and notes by James R. Newman,* Section 6, New York, 1966, pp. 603–19 illustrated with seven plates.

4. The main thesis of this essay—the duality of rational and irrational currents which so often appear simultaneously in English art and literature—seemed to Panofsky to be neatly summed up in the ecstatic female art nouveau figure on the solemn Doric radiator of the Rolls-Royce. The hypothesis had engaged him ever since his Hamburg days. He inscribed a copy of this article (significantly, it seemed to me), "Recorded from dark recollection."

5. We should, naturally, beware of oversimplification. There are six calico-bound notebooks, written in longhand, with many diagrams, which, in the summer vacation of the year 1911, Panofsky filled with excerpts from the over 1,200 pages of Theodor Lipps's works: *Grundlegung der Aesthetik* [part I of *Aesthetik. Psychologie des Schönen und der Kunst,* Hamburg and Leipzig, 1903], and *Die ästhetische Betrachtung und die bildende Kunst,* ibid. 1906. Similarly he worked through Immanuel Kant's *Kritik der reinen Vernunft.*

6. It might be rewarding to the student of Panofsky's work method to catalogue some of the reference works that visitors to 97 Battle Road will recall as being constantly on hand to be consulted in the midst of a lively conversation. Most important of all was quite possibly Brockhaus, *Conversations-Lexicon,* Leipzig, 1882; a close second was Salomon Reinach, *Répertoires,* followed by Carl Friederichs and Paul Wolters, *Die Gipsabgüsse antiker Bildwerke in historischer Folge erklärt,* Berlin, 1885; Andrea Alciati, *Emblemata,* Lyons, 1600; several mythological reference works—above all Daremberg and Saglio, *Dictionnaire des antiquités grecques et romaines* in 5 vols., Paris, 1877–1919—as well as the mythographic handbooks of Vincenzo Cartari and Natale Conti. A three-volume Benedictine edition of the Vulgate of the year 1737 in folio with impressive indices was one of the last books Panofsky consulted. *Idea* has recently been

issued in an English translation by Joseph J. S. Peake and Victor A. Velen (University of South Carolina Press, 1968)—a cause of genuine delight to its author.

7. Professor Wind kindly permitted me to quote from his letter of November 3, 1968.

8. "Now, of course, the term 'iconology' has lost some of its usefulness and most of its necessity owing to the very fact that no person in his right mind thinks of iconography in terms of a mere statistical and ancillary investigation" (September 3, 1967).

9. A list of student publications resulting from Panofsky's seminars is given in the separate printing of this lecture, appendices II and III. [See Publication Notes.—Ed.]

10. A splendid appraisal appeared not long ago in France: Roland Recht, "La méthode iconologique d'Erwin Panofsky," *Critique*, 24, March, 1968, pp. 315–23; see also the important essay by Erik Forssman, "Ikonologie und allgemeine Kunstgeschichte," *Zeitschrift für Aesthetik und Allgemeine Kunstwissenschaft*, 11, 2, 1967, pp. 132–69.

11. Letter of April 22, 1957. The German translation of *Tomb Sculpture* (Cologne, 1964) was undertaken by Professor L. L. Möller, the last, youngest, and most talented of Panofsky's German students in Hamburg. He wrote to her on November 6, 1964: "In sum, while I am still very skeptical of the value of the book as such, the German edition, based on your admirable translation, is what might be called the lesser of two evils. Let me thank you once more for all the time and effort you have spent on this ill-begotten child."

12. Panofsky took such delight in the movies that in 1946–47 he traveled to various places in and around Princeton, to give his talk as a *tema con variazioni*. He would end by showing one of his favorite silent films, such as Buster Keaton's *The Navigator*, which he would accompany with an extremely funny running commentary. When asked how he had arrived at his ideas about motion pictures, he said (February 1947) that he had gone to movies and liked some and disliked others and had fallen to thinking why, and then tried to capture the essence of it. He objected to Olivier's *Henry V* and to *The Cabinet of Dr. Caligari* on the grounds that reality had been sacrificed for the sake of artificiality. He defined the cinema's essential problem as "the manipulation of reality *as is*."

13. Relata refero. Professor von Blanckenhagen has another version of the Marienbad background which I shall leave to him to divulge, for the sake of historical

precision. I see to my delight that Goethe and the *Marienbader Elegie* are referred to by Panofsky in his *Problems in Titian*, New York, 1969, p. 23f. and note 35.

14. Panofsky reviewed this work in *Art Bulletin* [Bibl. 132], in itself a rare enough event, commending its author as "a lexicographer who is essentially a humanist . . . and the very fact that he is single-handedly undertaking a task Herculean in spite of its limitation to secular art not only gives unity and a delightful personal touch to his work but also promises well for its speedy consummation. . . . In the hands of big organizations rather than courageous individuals works of encyclopedic scholarship have a way of aiming at completeness without ever getting completed."

15. He was fascinated by the fact that the real Arcadia was a wild and savage province where human sacrifice was still being practiced in the days of the Roman Empire.

Illustrations

"What Is Baroque?" by Erwin Panofsky

"Style and Medium in the Motion Pictures" by Erwin Panofsky

"On the Ideological Antecedents of the Rolls-Royce Radiator" by Erwin Panofsky

"Erwin Panofsky: A Curriculum Vitae" by William S. Heckscher

Publication Notes

"Introduction" by Irving Lavin. Shorter version published as "Panofskys Humor" in German in Erwin Panofsky, *Die ideologischen Vorläufer des Rolls-Royce-Kühlers & Stil und Medium im Film. Mit Beiträgen von Irving Lavin und William S. Heckscher* (Frankfurt/New York: Campus Verlag, 1993), 7–15. Copyright by the author.

"What Is Baroque?" Previously unpublished lecture. Copyright by Irving Lavin.

"Style and Medium in the Motion Pictures." First published with the title "On Movies" in *Princeton University. Department of Art and Archaeology. Bulletin* (June 1936): 5–15. The enlarged version printed here was first published, with the present title, in *Critique* 1 (3) (1947): 5–28. Copyright by Gerda Panofsky.

"The Ideological Antecedents of the Rolls-Royce Radiator." Previously published in *Proceedings of the American Philosophical Society* 107 (1963): 273–88. Copyright by Gerda Panofsky.

"Erwin Panofsky: A Curriculum Vitae" by William S. Heckscher. German translation published in *Die ideologischen Vorläufer des Rolls-Royce-Kühlers & Stil und Medium im Film. Mit Beiträgen von Irving Lavin und William S. Heckscher* (Frankfurt/New York: Campus Verlag, 1993), 97–124. First published in *Record of the Art Museum. Princeton University* 28 (1969): 5–21. Also printed separately as *Erwin Panofsky: A Curriculum Vitae. a paper read at a symposium held at Princeton University on March 15, 1969, to mark the first anniversary of Erwin Panofsky's death,* Department of Art and Archaeology, Princeton University, Princeton, 1969, with appendixes listing dissertations and publications by Panofsky's students, and honors, distinctions, and festschriften he received. Reprinted in William S. Heckscher, *Art and Literature. Studies in Relationship,* ed. E. Verheyen (Baden-Baden: Verlag Valentin Koerner, 1985), 339–55. Copyright by William S. Heckscher.

About the Authors

Irving Lavin, born in 1927, was a student in Panofsky's courses in the early 1950s at New York University, and is his successor as Professor of Art History at the Institute for Advanced Study in Princeton. Lavin is the author of important works on the art of late antiquity, the Renaissance, and the Baroque, especially Bernini. His most recent book is *Past-Present. Essays on Historicism in Art from Donatello to Picasso* (Berkeley: University of California Press, 1993).

Erwin Panofsky, 1892–1968, was one of the most important art historians of this century. The necrology in this volume by his student and friend, William S. Heckscher, gives an account of his life. The MIT Press is the distributor of Erwin Panofsky, *Perspective as Symbolic Form,* translated by Christopher S. Wood (New York: Zone Books, 1991).

William S. Heckscher, born in 1904, was a student of Panofsky's in Hamburg and in 1936 followed him to Princeton. Heckscher taught art history in England, Canada, the Netherlands, and the United States, ultimately at Duke University. He is the author of *Rembrandt's "Anatomy of Dr. Nicholaas Tulp": An Iconological Study* (New York: New York University Press, 1958), and many essays on iconology and emblematics.

Name Index

Page numbers in italics indicate illustrations.